# Life is Good: 250 Anecdotes and Stories

David Bruce

Published by David Bruce, 2024.

While every precaution has been taken in the preparation of this book, the publisher assumes no responsibility for errors or omissions, or for damages resulting from the use of the information contained herein.

LIFE IS GOOD: 250 ANECDOTES AND STORIES

**First edition. November 1, 2024.**

Copyright © 2024 David Bruce.

ISBN: 979-8224534654

Written by David Bruce.

# Table of Contents

Chapter 1: From Ad-libs to Cartoons ............... 1
Chapter 2: From Children to Fights ............... 20
Chapter 3: From Food to Language ............... 42
Chapter 4: From Letters to Poetry ............... 65
Chapter 5: From Practical Jokes to Work ............... 85
Appendix A: Bibliography ............... 108
Appendix B: The Best Letter I Have Ever Received ............... 116
Appendix C: About the Author ............... 118
Appendix D: Some Books by David Bruce ............... 119

**On the Cover of *Life is Good: 250 Anecdotes and Stories*: Bob Montalto**

## Dedicated to Amateur and Professional Creative People

Rise above.

Theater director Tyrone Guthrie advised his actors and crew to do this. The advice means to rise above whatever forces are working against you. All of us have personal problems. No one's life is perfect. Sometimes, life seems to conspire against us. Rise above all that, and produce the best work you can.

Astonish me.

Dance impresario Sergei Diaghilev advised his choreographers to do this. The advice means what it says. Do such good work that the person who commissioned the work — and of course the audience — is astonished. (Tyrone Guthrie also used this phrase.)

Do it now.

As a young man, choreographer George Balanchine nearly died and so he believed in living his life day by day and not holding anything back. He would tell his dancers, "Why are you stingy with yourselves? Why are you holding back? What are you saving for — for another time? There are no other times. There is only now. Right now." Throughout his career, including before he became world renowned, he worked with what he had, not complaining about wanting a bigger budget or better dancers. One of the pieces of advice Mr. Balanchine gave over and over was this: "Do it now."

Go out and get one.

Ruth St. Denis once taught Martha Graham an important lesson when Ms. Graham was just starting to dance. Ms. St. Denis told Ms. Graham, "Show me your dance." Ms. Graham replied, "I don't have one," and Ms. St. Denis advised, "Well, dear, go out and *get* one." (Everyone needs an art to practice. Your art need not be dance. Perhaps your art can be writing autobiographical essays. Of course, you may practice more than one art.)

Assign yourself.

The parents of Marian Wright Edelman were serious about education. Each school night, she and her siblings were expected to sit down and do their homework. Whenever one of the children said that the teacher had not assigned any homework, her father used to say, "Well, assign yourself." Ms. Edelman once made out a list of "Twenty-Five Lessons for Life," based on the values she had learned from her parents. Lesson 3 was, "Assign yourself. Don't wait around to be told what to do." In 1973, she founded the Children's Defense Fund, which attempts to get federal legislation passed to help children.

Challenge yourself.

Joss Whelon created the TV series *Buffy the Vampire Slayer*, which is noted for its clever dialogue. Day after day, people told Joss that they watched the series because of its dialogue, so he decided to challenge himself by writing an episode in which the characters could not talk. The episode, titled "Hush," is excellent and was nominated for an Emmy.

Practice an art.

The father of choreographer Bella Lewitzky taught her the importance of having an art to practice. He worked at an ordinary job, but when he came home, he painted. Ms. Lewitzky says, "He taught me that it didn't make a d*mn bit of difference what you did for a living, as long as you had something that rewarded your life." He also didn't feel that it was necessary to have an audience for his art because the act of creation was rewarding in itself. Bella and her sister used to steal their father's paintings — because if they didn't, he would paint another work of art on top of the one he had already created.

Do it yourself.

Early in their career, the Ramones played in London on July 4, 1976. Some cool kids who called themselves The Clash hung around during a sound check before the concert and talked to the members of the band, mentioning that they played music but weren't good enough to play in public. Johnny Ramone told them, "Are you kidding? I hope you're coming tonight. We're lousy. We can't play. If you wait until you can play, you'll be too old to get up there. We stink, really. But it's great." (This is a great example of punk rock's do-it-yourself attitude. You don't need a lot of fancy equipment to play music. Just teach yourself a few chords, get up on stage, and rock. Similarly, if you want to write, you don't need a lot of fancy equipment. If you have a computer, great, but all you really need is some paper and a pencil or pen.)

Be there.

After retiring from her career in dance, Balanchine dancer Barbara Milberg became a very good student — and eventually a Ph.D. (and professor). In dance, she had learned that when the curtain went up, she had better be there, and so she never handed in a paper late.

Get it right.

A man — who didn't dance — visited the dance class of Margaret Craske. At the end of her class, he said goodbye and jokingly executed a *port de bras*. Quickly, Ms. Craske reached out and corrected the position of the visitor's hand. As you would expect, in her dance classes, she tells her students over and over, "Get it right!"

Do it 'til you get it right.

Garth Fagan, the choreographer of the theatrical version of *The Lion King*, learned an important lesson from choreographer Martha Graham: "Do it 'til you get it right!" She requested that he simply walk across the floor. He did 12 times before he realized that she wanted a walk that did not say, "LOOK AT ME!

AREN'T I GORGEOUS!" When he did the walk correctly, Ms. Graham told him, "I think you're going to go places." As the head of his own dance troupe and as a Broadway choreographer, he did.

Make the first mark.

Barbara Feldon, who played the role of Agent 99 on TV's *Get Smart*, is friends with artist Jan Stussy, whom she calls "the most prolific artist" she knows. She once asked him about his creation of art, "How did you develop the courage?" He replied, "When I was in the 10th grade, I realized that if you simply make the first mark, the rest will just happen. Whether it's that first mark with a brush on a canvas or pencil to paper, boldly make it and then let yourself free-fall. Art creates art." Ms. Feldon, author of *Living Alone and Loving It*, has added writing to her other creative endeavors, and she often tells herself, "Make the first mark."

# Chapter 1: From Ad-libs to Cartoons

**Ad-libs**

• Comedian Steve Allen was quick witted. He used to do a live television commercial in which he demonstrated the strength of a Fiberglass chair by banging on it with a hammer. One night, the chair broke when he hit it, and he quipped, "That's right, ladies and gentlemen, this hammer is made of Fiberglass." On another occasion, while he was live, a woman sitting in the balcony shouted down at him and asked if she could have his autograph. He shouted back, "Only if you have a very long pencil." He once asked a woman her name, and she told him, "Mrs. Holt. H-O-L-T." He replied, "Very well. W-E-L-L." Some people thought that he was setting up people for laughs, but he pointed out that often he played straight man to the people he interviewed. For example, he once asked a man his name, and although he was a professional comedian, he could not come up with an answer as funny as the answer the man gave: "Boston, Massachusetts."[1]

• Pete Barbutti is a musician as well as a comedian, and one of his routines is of a cool musician who plays a broom. In one routine, he announces that he will play "Tenderly," and then, accompanied by real musicians, he uses the broom to play, yes, "Tenderly." On the second chorus, he uses a cup as a mute for the broom. Once, he could not find his broom, so he sent his musician friends out to search the club for a broom. One of his friends found a vacuum cleaner and brought it to Mr. Barbutti just to see how he would react. He looked at it, sneered, and said, "No, man. I don't play Fender broom."[2]

• Frank Sinatra tipped well — extremely well — but he demanded good service. He once invited his husband-and-wife friends Don and Barbara Rickles to a dinner party to celebrate their second anniversary. Everything was wonderful: the cold Jack Daniels, the hot hors d'oeuvers, a magnificent Chinese dinner. Well, almost wonderful. The service was slow, and this got on Frank's nerves. And when a server dropped noodles onto Frank's lap, Frank tipped the table over and left. The Rickles were left covered in Chinese food. Barbara rose to the occasion. She pointed to the glass of vodka that she was holding in her hand and asked, "Waiter, could I have some more ice?" (Frank sent Barbara a note of apology the next day.)

Frank Sinatra could be prickly with people he did not like, although he was a good friend to his friends. Don Rickles saw him come into a club one night and told him, "Make yourself comfortable, Frank. Hit someone." And when a (former?) fan hit Frank one night, a critic remarked, "That's the first time the fan hit the sh*t."[3]

- *The Chicago Sun-Times* was a crowded place to work. Ann Landers, whose real name was Eppie Lederer, had a desk in a room filled with many other desks, each with a reporter working at it. Her desk was next to the desk of Paul Molloy, the TV-radio critic. One day, Mr. Molloy was working at his desk while talking on a telephone headset. He tipped his chair too far, fell backwards, lay on the floor, and kept on talking. Eppie Lederer looked at him, then dug a pamphlet out of one of her files, and handed it to him. The pamphlet had this title: "Drinking Problem? Take This Test of Twenty Questions."[4]

- Entertainer Sammy Davis Jr. had only one eye. He and comedian Joey Bishop once drove from Los Angeles to Las Vegas. Mr. Davis was driving 90 miles per hour when a police officer pulled him over. When the police officer asked if he knew how fast he was going, Mr. Davis said, "Around 70." The police officer said, "Seventy? You were way over that. You were going at least 90." Mr. Bishop interrupted: "Officer, the man has one eye. Do you want him to look at the road or at the speedometer?"[5]

- Some comedians are funny all the time, not just while they are on stage. Comedian Shelley Berman once said that Jonathan Winters was "the most 'on' comedian I know." Mr. Winters proved that in 1988: He collapsed, and a male paramedic had to give him mouth-to-mouth resuscitation to revive him. When Mr. Winters regained consciousness, the first thing he did was to tell the paramedic, "You're a very attractive man."[6]

• Comedian Groucho Marx knew how to ad-lib. Once when he was booed, he told the audience, "I have to stay here — I'm getting paid. But nobody's keeping you." Of course, the audience laughed at the ad-lib, and then the audience started to laugh at Groucho's jokes.[7]

• Comedian Shecky Greene once drove his car into a fountain at Caesar's Palace in Las Vegas. When the police looked in the car window to see if he was OK, he joked, "No spray wax, please."[8]

**Alcohol**

• *The Chicago Sun-Times* was a crowded place to work. Ann Landers, whose real name was Eppie Lederer, had a desk in a room filled with many other desks, each with a reporter working at it. Her desk was next to the desk of Paul Molloy, the TV-radio critic. One day, Mr. Molloy was working at his desk while talking on a telephone headset. He tipped his chair too far, fell backwards, lay on the floor, and kept on talking. Eppie Lederer looked at him, then dug a pamphlet out of one of her files, and handed it to him. The pamphlet had this title: "Drinking Problem? Take This Test of Twenty Questions."[9]

• In 1982, Ray Bradbury, age 62, took his first flight in an airplane. Normally, while traveling he took a passenger train across land or an ocean liner across sea, but he was attending the opening of EPCOT Center in Florida as a guest of The Walt Disney Company, and his passenger train trip home to California was suddenly cancelled. He asked The Walt Disney Company to buy him a plane ticket home, give him three double martinis, and "pour him on the plane." All went well. He discovered that he was not actually afraid of flying — he was afraid of being afraid of flying and of doing such things as running up and down the aisles, screaming. In his later years, he frequently flew.[10]

• Archibald MacLeish won three Pulitzer prizes: two for poetry and one for drama. At Harvard, he taught English SA, an exclusive creative writing course. Financial writer Scott Burns remembers that at the first class, Mr. MacLeish stated that it was good to have a few drinks while discussing poetry, and then he brought out bottles of bourbon, scotch, and vodka. Mr. Burns remembers, "He urged us to stretch and to risk failure. So I did. I'm embarrassed about every word written in that period, but I found that you could survive failure, particularly if you do it a lot."[11]

- Ralph Steadman, who illustrated some of Hunter S. Thompson's books, including *Fear and Loathing in Las Vegas*, tells a story of taking Mr. Thompson to a pub in Kent, England: "He asked for whisky and the guy behind the bar served him a single measure. Hunter stared at it, and then he looked at me and asked, 'What the hell is this? A free sample?'"[12]

- Penn & Teller once wrote a number of anti-drunk-driving ads — Penn & Teller are both teetotalers. In one ad, Penn said, "If your friend wants to drive drunk, take his keys and while you're at it, take his wallet. He won't notice — he's drunk!" In another, Penn said, "If you're going to kill someone, use a knife. Then you can pick who you want to kill and you can enjoy it. Don't drive drunk."[13]

- Harpo Marx once visited W.C. Fields, who showed him around his home. The pool table had a cushion because on nights when he couldn't sleep in bed he would sleep on the pool table, and his cellar was stocked with hundreds of cases of different kinds of alcohol because, Mr. Fields explained, "Never can be sure Prohibition won't come back, my boy."[14]

- Monty Python member Graham Chapman battled alcoholism much of the time. After he remodeled his home in Highgate so that it had a wine cellar, he stocked it entirely with his favorite alcoholic drink, gin, so he ended up with a gin — not wine — cellar. By the way, *Monty Python's Big Red Book* (1971) has a blue cover.[15]

**Animals**

- Comedian Fred Allen knew a small-time vaudevillian who acquired enough money to buy a chicken farm and retire.

Unfortunately, the vaudevillian missed the excitement of entertaining people and did not enjoy the lack of excitement of raising chickens. Mr. Allen visited the retired vaudevillian one day and listened to him complain. Around them were dozens of white chickens, each of which had a round red spot on its behind. To Mr. Allen, the sight reminded him of dozens of Japanese flags. The retired vaudevillian explained what had happened. He had been giving the chickens a special feed to make them lay larger eggs. The special feed worked — the chickens had been laying eggs so large that they wrecked the chickens' egg-laying equipment. The retired vaudevillian complained, "I had to catch every lousy hen and dab her behind with Mercurochrome [a red medicine]!"

Speaking of edible birds, a butcher friend of vaudevillian comedian Jack Inglis gave him a plumb turkey in early October to eat for Thanksgiving. Unfortunately, Mr. Inglis' children enjoyed playing with and chasing the turkey, and in the seven weeks before Thanksgiving, the turkey ran so much that it lost 20 pounds. Mr. Inglis' fellow comedian and friend Fred Allen wrote, "For their Thanksgiving Day dinner that year, the Inglis family had what looked like a tall sparrow."[16]

• Whenever strangers who are traveling on a train or airplane ask Carol O'Connor, author of the mystery series starring the anti-social character Mallory, what she does for a living, she replies, "I kill people." She says that this response elicits "a short conversation, no eye contact, and no sudden movement by my seatmate, only peace and quiet." Why does she write about sudden death? She points out, "Violent death is larger than life. And it's the great equalizer. By law, every victim is entitled to a paladin and a chase, else life would be cheapened." Interestingly, a copy editor once thanked her for only wounding a pet in a book instead of doing what she usually did and killing it. Ms. O'Connor says, "Apparently I can murder all the people I want. No one minds that. But the first time an animal died (on the first page of my first book), it generated anxious mail."[17]

- As you may expect, Beatrix Potter, the creator of Peter Rabbit, collected odd animal tales from the *Times* of London. One such tale was about a widower who was alone except for his cat. The two dined together at the same table. The two each had chairs, and the two each had plates. The widower would take food from his own plate and put it on the cat's plate, and then the two would eat. One day, the cat was late for a meal, and the widower worried. Soon, however, the cat arrived, carrying two dead mice. The cat put one dead mouse on her own plate, and she put one dead mouse on the widower's plate.[18]

**Audiences**

- William T. Vollmann has written fiction and nonfiction of an astounding length. He worked for 23 years on his treatise on violence, *Rising Up and Rising Down: Some Thoughts on Violence, Freedom and Urgent Means*, which clocks in at 3,352 pages. As of 2022, five of the novels of his seven-cycle novel titled *Seven Dreams: A Book of North American Landscapes* had been completed. An interviewer once asked him, "Continuing to adhere to a Tolstoian vision of the novel — its immensity, grandeur, complexity and size — how have you been able to survive in the marketplace with an uncompromising vision completely outside of the mainstream?" Mr. Vollmann replied, "When I write my books, I don't care about the marketplace."[19]

- Comedian Doug Stanhope dislikes the warm-ups the audiences of TV shows are put through before the show begins. These warm-ups are designed to make audiences wildly enthusiastic, and these warm-ups work. Mr. Stanhope went on one TV show, and the crowd was wildly enthusiastic. Being a comedian, Mr. Stanhope punctures pretensions, so he said, "It sounds like all my fans are here!" The audience was wildly enthusiastic: "YEEEEAHH!" Then Mr. Stanhope asked, "Then what's my name?" How did the audience react? Mr. Stanhope says, "F\*\*king dead silence." He also says that the TV show edited that part out.[20]

**Authors**

- James Thurber, a remarkable master of humorous short stories that were published in *The New Yorker*, had a remarkable memory, which he inherited from his mother, and he could remember the birthdays of a couple of hundred people. He also could remember conversations that had taken place many years ago. Robert M. Coates, author of the novel *The Eater of Darkness*, once could not remember the subject of a conversation that he had had long ago with Stephen Vincent Benét, but Mr. Thurber said that he knew the topic of conversation. Mr. Coates replied that Mr. Thurber had not been present and therefore could not possibly know the topic of conversation. Mr. Thurber pointed out, "You happened to mention it in passing about twelve years ago. You were arguing about a play called *Swords*." Mr. Thurber was correct; however, he says, "But it's strange to reach a position where your friends have to be supplied with their own memories. It's bad enough dealing with your own."

Of course, Mr. Thurber had many memories of Harold Ross, editor of *The New Yorker*. Mr. Ross once sent his employees a memo in a sealed envelope; the memo stated, "When you send me a memorandum with four-letter words in it, seal it. There are women in this office." Mr. Thurber's reaction was this: "Yeah, Ross, and they know a lot more of these words than you do." And when Mr. and Mrs. Thurber were in Mr. Ross' office, Mr. Ross told them about a man and a woman, "I have every reason to believe that they're s-l-e-e-p-i-n-g together." Mrs. Thurber's reaction was this: "Why, Harold Ross, what words you do spell out." Mr. Thurber says, "But honest to goodness, that was genuine. Women are either good or bad, he once told me, and the good ones must not hear these things.

Mr. Thurber once met author Frank Harris, who hung on a wall the portraits of — in his opinion — the three greatest American writers. His portrait was in the middle, and he told Mr. Thurber, "Those three are the best American writers. The one in the middle is the best." Another author with a foible was Thomas Wolfe, who wrote huge novels and who thought that real writers wrote huge novels. Mr. Thurber said, "Wolfe once told me at a cocktail party that I didn't know what it was to be a writer. My wife, standing next to me, complained about that. 'But my husband is a writer,' she said. Wolfe was genuinely surprised. 'He is?' he asked. 'Why, all I ever see is that stuff of his in *The New Yorker*."[21]

• Jo Nesbø is the Norwegian author of Scanda-noir crime thrillers starring the character Harry Hole, about whose last name he said, "The Norwegian pronunciation is Hoola, but it's fine if you call him Hole." When Mr. Nesbø was younger, he played in a rock band with a younger brother. Mr. Nesbø said, "When we started the band, we really weren't that good and we would change our name every week so that audiences wouldn't realize it was us playing again. So the band never really had a name. Eventually we got a bit better and fans would ask when *di derre* [Norwegian for 'those guys'] were coming back. So we called ourselves Di Derre." Mr. Nesbø is a soccer [European football] fan. When he was 10 years old, he thought about becoming a fan of the Arsenal football club, but an older brother forced him to become a fan of Tottenham. Mr. Nesbø explained, "I had been thinking about supporting Arsenal because I quite liked the shirts. But then my 15-year-old brother told me firmly that I wasn't [going to support Arsenal] and that I had two days to learn the entire Tottenham squad. He wasn't someone that you disobeyed." Harry Hole is a fan of Tottenham Hotspur football club, and in one of Mr. Nesbø's Harry Hole thrillers, the bad guys are drug dealers who wear Arsenal replica shirts. Mr. Nesbø said, "I've got a number of friends who support Arsenal, and they gave me a lot of grief about that. They said, 'Only a coward uses his power as a writer to do something like that.' [...] I told them to sod off."[22]

• Daniel Pinkwater has written lots of books, including many books for kids. He says about himself (using the third person), "Daniel Pinkwater is crazy about writing, and has been trying to learn how to do it for 50 years. He has written about a hundred books, all but two or three of them good." Among other things, he is a good interview subject. For example, when asked, "What fictional character would you like to be your friend, and why?," he replied, "Moby Dick, because except for Ishmael he is the only character who does not get killed at the end of the book, and having a gigantic white whale for a friend would be cool."

Daniel's most memorable teacher was a man named Thrasher Hall, who taught summer school and was excited about literature. He also communicated his excitement to his students. Daniel remembers another student in the class: Hiram. This student was not rich, as he had only one white shirt, which his loving mother would wash and iron each night so he could wear it again the next day. Daniel says, "One day, he turned up with a paperback copy of *Macbeth* which he had bought himself. I asked him why he had spent money on the book when Mr. Hall gave us daily installments of the play via phonograph records. Hiram said he couldn't wait to find out how the story came out."

By the way, when Daniel was a kid, guess what he wanted to be when he grew up? "The greatest swordsman in France."[23]

• Herman Melville, author of *Moby-Dick; or, The Whale*, found a four-leaf clover the day he got married; of course, he considered it a sign that his marriage would be a happy one. (The two stayed married, despite financial difficulties.) He wrote two of his books simply to please the public and to make money: *Redburn: His First Voyage* and *White-Jacket; or, The World in a Man-of-War*. When an English magazine gave *Redburn* a long, thoughtful review, Mr. Melville wrote — privately, in his journal — that he found it surprising that the editor was willing to "waste so many pages upon a thing which I, the author, know to be trash, and wrote it to buy some tobacco with." During his voyage to England, Mr. Melville was pleased to see someone reading a copy of one of his books: *Omoo: A Narrative of Adventures in the South Seas*. When Mr. Melville died, his work as an author was nearly forgotten. His *New York Times* obituary stated that his name was Henry Melville and that his best book was his first one: *Typee: A Peep at Polynesia Life*. If Raymond Weaver, a professor of English and comparative literature at Columbia University, had not gotten permission from Mr. Melville's family to look through his papers, Mr. Melville might be completely forgotten today. Mr. Weaver found the unpublished manuscript *Billy Budd* and contributed to the Melville Revival of the 1920s that led to Mr. Melville being considered one of the United States' greatest novelists.[24]

• Sometimes, it was hard to get an interview with Canadian novelist Ernest Buckler, author of *The Mountain and the Valley*. The shy writer once hid in the cornfields of his farm rather than be interviewed. He did find living in a rural area conducive to being a writer, although the country did have its own kind of distractions. He needed silence to write, and he once said that sometimes when he was ready to write "this is precisely the time when somebody will come in, some gal, you know, who'll talk for hours on end as to whether her husband prefers turnips in the stew or cauliflower." Although Mr. Buckler was shy, he was a good interview. He once said, "Writers, by and large, are the dreariest people you can possibly know, because they are just stuffed with words, like dry-bread dressing on a Christmas Eve goose's ass." As a famous author, he sometimes received funny letters. Someone from Cape Breton wrote him, "I enjoyed your book very much. It was such clear print." A woman from Seattle, Washington, sent him her measurements and wrote him that his name — Ernest Redmond Buckler — thrilled her and that she could see him on a white charger rescuing damsels in distress. Mr. Buckler said, "My God, myself on a white charger! I'm scared sh*tless of horses. One kicked me in the head at thirteen."[25]

• Isabel Allende, an author from Chile, has been living an interesting life. When she was a child living in Lebanon (her stepfather was a diplomat), bullets flew in the streets because of religious and political conflicts. Her family set up mattresses in the windows, and they decided, of course, to send Isabel and her brothers home to Chile. One of her first jobs was translating romance novels; however, she is a feminist, and because she found the heroines of the romance novels she was translating to be passive, she changed some passages to make the heroines more active. When these changes were discovered, she lost that job. Of course, she became the author of such books as *The House of the Spirits* and *Eva Luna*, and she occasionally becomes annoyed by the literary analysis that scholars do on her books. She once said, "Often, I visit universities and I find there is a group of thirty youngsters whom they have tortured during the semester looking for symbols and metaphors in a book of mine where there were no symbols or metaphors intended — where all I intended was to tell the story. I ask them why they don't yield to the pleasure of reading in the same way that I yield to the pleasure of writing instead of analyzing and forcing parallels, and searching for influences.[26]

• Isaac Asimov wrote hundreds of books. Asked what his favorite book is, he used to reply, "The last one I've written." Of course, he was known for writing science fiction, but he also wrote many books about science for the general public. He once said, "I can read a dozen dull books and make one interesting book out of them." Other people wondered how he could write so much. (He did it by writing for hours every day.) Mr. Asimov did not get a word processor until June of 1981, preferring to write on typewriters. While interviewing Mr. Asimov in 1982, Frank Kendig joked, "I think most of us thought that you had one [a word processor] all along — that or a team of writers chained in the basement." Many people have rituals such as sharpening pencils that they perform before they begin to write. Mr. Asimov once said, "The only thing I do before I start writing is to make sure that I'm close enough to the typewriter to reach the keys." An interviewer once asked Mr. Asimov what he would do if he were told that he had only six months to live. He replied, "Type faster!"[27]

- Ray Bradbury remembered being presented with the Medal for Distinguished Contribution to American Letters as "a fantastic evening"; however, he did run into a problem. Late in the evening, heading back to his room, he suddenly felt an urgent need to pee. He said, "For God's sake, where's the men's room?" None was handy, but fortunately a woman said, "There's a potted palm over there. Why don't you go use it?" Mr. Bradbury said, "Nobody saw me. At least I don't think so." One of Mr. Bradbury's most famous works is *Fahrenheit 451*, which is about a fireman who does not put out fires, but instead starts them in order to burn books. Mr. Bradbury, of course, loved books. He said, "I'm completely library educated. I've never been to college. I went down to the library when I was in grade school in Waukegan, and in high school in Los Angeles, and spent long days every summer in the library." He also used to steal magazines from a store, wash his hands, read the magazines, and then sneak them back into the store and put them back where they belonged. Mr. Bradbury's lifelong credo was this: "Jump off the cliff and build your wings on the way down."[28]
- Gwendolyn Brooks, a poet who won the Pulitzer Prize, was a big fan of soap operas and would not talk on the telephone when a favorite soap opera was being broadcast. Her daughter, Nora, once called her, and Gwendolyn picked up the receiver, immediately said, "*All My Children*," and hung up. By the way, Nora's parents met at a party, Gwendolyn said, when "this glorious man appeared in the doorway and posed for a moment, looking the situation over." She remembered, "I was always impressed by dignity in a man, and he certainly had that." Gwendolyn was so impressed by the man, whose name was Henry Lowington Blakely Jr., that she told her friend Margaret Taylor, "That's the man I'm going to marry." Margaret immediately yelled at the man, "Hey, boy, this girl wants to meet you." The couple's other child was a son, named Henry after his father. Young Henry spent a long time getting to bed because he said goodnight to everybody, including his fish (Water Boy) and his puppy (Cocoa).[29]

- As a young man, William Faulkner became friends with Sherwood Anderson. Before noon, Mr. Faulkner would never see Mr. Anderson, but in the afternoon they would walk together around New Orleans and talk to people, and in the evening they would share a bottle or two of an alcoholic beverage and Mr. Faulkner would listen as Mr. Anderson talked. Mr. Faulkner decided that if this was the life of a writer, then the life of a writer was the life for him. He began writing his first novel, and he discovered that he liked writing. After about three weeks of Mr. Faulkner not seeing Mr. Anderson, Mr. Anderson showed up at Mr. Faulkner's home and asked him, "Are you mad at me?" Mr. Faulkner replied that he was writing his first novel. Mr. Anderson said, "My God!" Then he left. Soon Mr. Faulkner finished his first novel, and Mr. Anderson's wife told him, "Sherwood says that he will make a trade with you. If he doesn't have to read your manuscript, he will tell his publisher to accept it." Mr. Faulkner said, "I said, 'Done,' and that's how I became a writer."[30]
- Dick Francis, who was a jockey before becoming the author of thrillers, did not bet on the horses. He explained, "I never bet. If I did, I'd watch only one horse. I prefer to watch the tactics of all the jockeys." A good interviewee as well as a good jockey and a good writer, Mr. Francis once told Franz Lidz why he started writing: "Because the carpets were getting thin, and my sons needed educating." He usually wrote one book per year, beginning the thriller in early January and finishing it in mid-May, when his publisher, Jenny Dereham of Michael Joseph, Ltd., would travel to the Caymans, where he lived much of the time. Mr. Francis once said, "She always says if I meet her at the airport she knows it's finished. If my wife meets her, I'm probably struggling with the last two paragraphs." Mr. Francis believed that writing does have one important advantage over riding in a race: "When a race is over, it's gone for good. A book remains."[31]
- Margaret Wise Brown, the author of the children's story "Goodnight Moon," was an eccentric. When she received her very first

royalty check, she bought every flower for sale on a flower cart. She owned land and a house in Maine that she referred to as "The Only House." Among other features, she had an outdoor room including a mirror nailed to a tree, a table, and a nightstand. She once decorated her room in a hotel in Paris with orange trees and live birds. Many of her friends were also eccentrics. They formed a group they called the Bird Brain Society. One of the rules was that a member could declare any day Christmas and invite the other members of the group to come over and celebrate. She died early, at age 42. Following an operation for appendicitis in France, she seemed to be recovering well. To show her nurse how well she was doing, she kicked her leg as if she were doing the can-can and died instantly of an embolism.[32]

• John McPhee loved sports when he was young, and his father was a doctor of sports medicine at Princeton. When John was eight years old, the football team gave him a Princeton football jersey, made by the same company that made the Princeton team's football uniforms; his number was 33. At games, he ran onto the field with the team. In addition, he says, "When Princeton scored a touchdown, I went behind the goalpost and caught the extra point." He also stayed on the sidelines during games; however, one cold, wet day he looked up at the press box and realized that the sportswriters were dry and in an environment with heaters. That is when he decided to be a writer. Mr. McPhee says, "Now that story, which I have often told, is about three to five percent apocryphal. The rest of it is absolutely true."[33]

• Photographer Nancy Crampton took a series of portraits of famous authors. She wanted to take a portrait of Philip Roth on a rural road, and they went from road from road as she tried to find exactly the right setting. Eventually, Mr. Roth grew tired of this and said to her, "Nancy, the road didn't write the book."[34]

**Bathrooms**

• The elderly become preoccupied with always knowing where a bathroom is located. Such was the case with the 82-year-old Norman

Mailer, who once was hurrying to a bathroom when fellow author Philip Roth asked him, "Where are you going in such a hurry, Norman?" Mr. Mailer replied, "Well, I have to tell you, Phil. I've got to urinate. When you get to my age, this becomes a desperate matter. In fact, let me warn you, when you get to my age, you're going to be looking around for telephone booths in which you can relieve yourself." Mr. Roth replied, "Norman, I'm already there."[35]

• In her memoir *I Love a Broad Margin to My Life*, Maxine Hong Kingston writes that Joseph, her grown son, reads all of her writing and has requested of her, "Don't write about me." She agreed, but later in the book she wrote that once when Joseph was very young she gave him a whole bag of marshmallows so she could write uninterrupted for 20 minutes. She also writes about how she and Alice Walker were arrested while protesting war. The result was that they were both handcuffed and put in jail. Ms. Kingston was forced to ask Ms. Walker to undo her pants for her so she could pee.[36]

• Early in his marriage, Dick King-Smith, the author of *Babe: The Gallant Pig*, on which the film *Babe* was based, and his wife lived in a house without an indoor bathroom. He used to bury the contents of the chamber pot in a field, which became a strange sight. Much of the field was an ordinary grass-green color, but it had a large number of very dark green spots.[37]

**Books**

• British author Stephen Benatar wrote for decades, but without much success. True, he did get some novels published, such as *The Man on the Bridge*. (His children helped by praying that Dad would find a publisher.) But despite good reviews, often he could not find a publisher for the novels that he kept producing because he so loved writing. This led to some creative problem-solving on his part. In fact, after *Such Men Are Dangerous* was rejected many times, he persuaded his local council — Scunthorpe Borough Council — to act as the publisher of the novel, despite this protest by a local Tory councilor: "It's the duty of the council to dispose of rubbish — not publish it!"

Eventually, he created his own imprint and republished his novels — and sold them himself. He often signs books at bookstores, and very often he will approach a stranger and say, "Hello, I'm signing copies of my novel. Would you be so kind as to take a look?" Then he shoves one of his books into the hands of the stranger and walks off. This approach works well. He says, "I remember one manager at a bookstore in Kingston saying, 'I'll eat my hat if you sell any copies here. My clientele aren't the type to go in for this sort of thing.' I sold a hundred copies that day."

Andrew Raymond from Waterstone's in Staines is amazed by Mr. Benatar's success in selling books: "He has a charismatic presence that people like. He sells around 50 books every time he comes in, which is a fantastic achievement for an unknown author." Mr. Benatar says, "My record is 128 books in one day. I actually outsold J.K. Rowling and John Grisham that day. But then, I was there, and they weren't." One day, he shoved a copy of *Wish Her Safe at Home* into the hands of Edwin Franks, the managing editor of the publishing section of *The New York Review of Books*. Mr. Franks read and loved the book. He says, "It was a lucky accident that I ran into Benatar — or should I say he ran into me? I read the book straight away and was knocked out. It's not every day you find a neglected classic from an Englishman who is still alive. Everyone in the office read it and was just as excited as I was."

The publishing section of *The New York Review of Books* published *Wish Her Safe at Home* and suddenly Mr. Benatar had a success, something unexpected by his children. Prue, his daughter, said, "I think we're all delighted but rather surprised by Dad's sudden success. We had to watch him all the time we were growing up, always writing and never getting anywhere. At the time we resented the fact that he wasn't spending more time with us and wasn't making enough money."

Eileen, his former wife, said, "I think it's great that he's at last being recognized. He has devoted his whole life to his books. I admit there were times when I thought he was wasting his time. He had the talent but not the luck. And now he's been vindicated."[38]

- The parents of Stephenie Meyer, who as an adult wrote *Twilight* after having a vivid dream about a girl and a male vampire talking in a meadow, wanted their children to be readers. When Stephenie was seven years old, in 1980, her father read to the children before they went to bed Terry Brooks' *The Sword of Shannara*. He would reach an exciting place and then stop reading for the night. Each day, Stephenie would sneak the book out of her parents' closet and read ahead to find out what had happened. The following year, her father began to read a chapter each night from *Gone with the Wind*. Once again, Stephenie would get the book out and read ahead. Of course, the *Twilight Saga* was a major success. Ms. Meyer was once asked whether her husband was jealous of Edward Cullen, the vampire. She replied, "No, he refuses to be jealous of fictional characters. He says, 'I'm real, so I've got one on him there.'" Ms. Meyer got a $750,000 advance for a book contract to publish *Twilight* and two more novels. She was happy. She said, "I'd been hoping for $10,000 to pay off my minivan."[39]

- As you would expect, Black poet Gwendolyn Brooks loved to read. In her old age, she walked into a bookstore and bought $300 worth of books. The sales person asked if she were buying for a library. Ms. Brooks replied, "No, I just like to read — it's just like climbing to the top of Mount Everest." She once said that she hoped that her poetry would give readers and listeners "nourishment or healing or just plain rich pleasure." By the way, as kids do, Ms. Brooks' two children — Henry and Nora — sometimes fought when they were young. When Nora had chicken pox, the children's father told Henry, "You can't hit your sister. She's sick." Young Henry replied, "No — but I can credit it to her account."[40]

- Ian Fleming, author of the James Bond books, had an important book collection, which consisted of books that contained new ideas. The ideas could be a description of a new invention or theory, or even a description of a game which was previously unknown. During World War II, the British government considered the books to be of national importance, and they were kept at the Bodleian Library in Oxford. After his first few James Bond books made him successful, Mr. Fleming bought a gold-plated typewriter, on which he typed the last James Bond books.[41]
- Ursula K. Le Guin had heard about Tolkien's *Lord of the Rings*, but she resisted reading it because of what she regarded as the *Saturday Review*'s "fulsome" reviews of the series of novels. Finally, she took out *The Fellowship of the Ring* from the Emory University library. She started reading it, and the next day she hurried back to the library, "in terrible fear" that the other volumes of the trilogy had been checked out. They hadn't, and she read constantly for the next few days.[42]
- Sometimes, even good writers sell few copies. Charlotte, Emily, and Anne Brontë, authors of *Jane Eyre*, *Wuthering Heights*, and the sustained feminist novel *The Tenant of Wildfell Hall*, once published *Poems by Currer, Ellis, and Acton Bell*, using these pseudonyms instead of their real names. They sold two copies.[43]

**Cartoons**

- When Tex Avery began working as a gag writer at the early Warner Brothers Cartoon Studio, he found himself in a group of other crazy people. The first time he met the other gag writers, they built a fire in the middle of the floor of the writing room and then sat around it like a group of Native Americans. One of the gag writers was Dave Monahan, who quit by saying, "I'm going to the dentist," and then driving from California to Florida to get a job at another studio. When Tex worked as a cartoon director for MGM, he created a sexy Red Riding Hood character. The first cartoon the character appeared in was "Red Hot Riding Hood," which appeared in 1943. Much of the humor resulted from the wolf character's exaggerated reactions to the sexy Red Riding Hood. The Hays Office censored a lot of the cartoon, so lots of funny stuff was taken out, but Tex and others at MGM learned from the experience. If they ever wanted a sexy character in one of their cartoons, they would add some other VERY sexy characters to the synopsis they sent to the Hays Office. The censors would censor the VERY sexy characters and leave in the sexy character that Tex wanted to use. By the way, MGM did some training films for the military. A military officer saw the uncensored version of "Red Hot Riding Hood" and requested that that version be sent to overseas American soldiers, with whom it was very popular. By the way, Tex once gambled with a boss, Leon Schlesinger. Tex ended up owing him $10, promised to pay it the following day, and as promised brought in $10. The money was all pennies, and all unrolled, and in a bag, which Tex emptied onto the floor.[44]

• Some cartoon characters such as Bugs Bunny have such strong personalities that they take on a life of their own and sometimes people forget they are fictional. For example, children sometimes object to anyone saying that illustrators draw Bugs Bunny. The children say that the illustrators draw *pictures of* Bugs Bunny — an important distinction. Bill Scott, who later became the voice of Bullwinkle of Rocky and Bullwinkle fame, once wrote his grandmother a letter in which he said that he wrote scripts for Bugs Bunny. His grandmother wrote back, "I don't see why you have to write scripts for Bugs Bunny. He's funny enough just the way he is."[45]

# Chapter 2: From Children to Fights

**Children**

• Roger Ebert wrote, "I was born at the center of the universe, and have had good fortune for all of my days. The center was located at the corner of Washington and Maple streets in Urbana, Illinois, a two-bedroom white stucco house with green canvas awnings, evergreens and geraniums in front and a white picket fence enclosing the back yard." Of course, he had many stories about growing up there:

1) He and his family ate meat loaf and green beans sometimes at a diner, but he remembers his first meal at a real restaurant: a Steak 'n' Shake, where his father ordered a hamburger for him. Young Roger said, "But I don't like ham." His father replied, "You'll like this ham."

2) In the basement of his home, young Roger operated his own small business: the Roger Ebert Stamp Company. He would sell "approvals" to a few customers who responded to his ten-cent advertisements in small stamp magazines. One day a couple of men came to his house, saying that they wanted to see his wares and might buy a few stamps. Young Roger took them to the basement and showed them his "approvals," but the men didn't buy anything. His father walked in as the men walked out and asked, "What did those men want?" He then said, "Their car said 'Department of Internal Revenue.'"

3) Roger's father was an electrician who worked at the University of Illinois. Lots of fathers let their sons see them work, and lots of sons end up doing the same kind of work that their fathers do. Roger's father never let Roger see him doing electrical work. Instead, he said, "Boy, I don't want you to become an electrician. I was working in the English Building today, and I saw those fellows with their feet up on their desks, smoking their pipes and reading their books. That's the job for you."[46]

• Comedian Alan Abel once received a caboose as payment for a roast of a train company's executives. Once he had the caboose, however, he had to find a way to convince the zoning commission to let him put it on his property. He told them he wanted to give his daughter a playhouse in the form of a caboose, and the commission asked how heavy the caboose playhouse was. Hearing that it weighed about 50 tons, the zoning commission told him no. He appealed the ruling, and at the appeal hearing he took his four-year-old daughter, Jennifer. Before they arrived at the hearing, he asked what she would do if the appeal was denied. She replied, "I'll cry," and he told her, "OK — just don't stop." The appeal was denied, Jennifer cried and cried and cried, and the zoning commission decided to let her have a caboose. The next problem was getting the caboose onto his property, which was four miles away. The only company that was able to move the caboose wanted to charge $1,000 a mile — too much. Therefore, he asked Jennifer how much money she had in her piggybank, a figure that turned out to be about $4. Together, they went to see a VIP at the company, who turned out to be a man with lots of photos of children and grandchildren on his walls. Jennifer told the VIP, "You can have all the money in my piggybank, and you can play in my caboose any time you want to, if you move it." The VIP then told Mr. Abel, "We'll move it for $400 instead of $4,000." Mr. Abel says, "And they did."[47]

- Eric Blair, who was later famous under the pseudonym George Orwell, liked books even as a young boy. The day before his 8th birthday, he found his mother's present to him: a copy of Jonathan Swift's *Gulliver's Travels*. Instead of waiting to be given the book, he took it and started reading it. One of his friends at St. Cyprian's school was Cyril Connolly. Both boys were fans of H.G. Wells, and when one boy got a copy of Mr. Wells' *The Country of the Blind*, they kept stealing it from each other so they could read it. Mr. Blair said later, "I can still remember at four o'clock on a midsummer morning, with the school fast asleep and the sun slanting through the window, creeping down a passage to Connolly's dormitory where I knew the book would be beside his bed." By the way, Eric's time at St. Cyprian's was not always pleasant. He used to grease his hair so that a mean schoolmistress could not easily pull it. Young Eric was a problem-solver in more ways than one: During a summer vacation, he found a way to befriend the Buddicom children: He stood on his head. When they asked why he was standing on his head, he replied, "You are noticed more if you stand on your head than if you are right way up."[48]

• On 21 July 1899, Ernest Hemingway was born. A neighbor, Mrs. Bagley, knew immediately that the Hemingways had a son because she woke up to the sound of a cornet. Ernest's father had told her that if his wife gave birth to a son, he would go out on his porch and play his cornet. Ernest's father, a doctor, also cooked. Once, during his rounds as a doctor, he called home and said that it was time to take out of the oven the pie he had made. In some ways, Ernest's parents were strict. In the 7th grade, Ernest was assigned by his teacher to read Jack London's violent novel *The Call of the Wild*. His mother went to the school and complained to his teacher, "It's not the kind of book young people should be reading." When Ernest played on the Sabbath, his father switched him with a leather strap and then made him kneel and pray to God for forgiveness. Ernest and a friend named Harold Sampson shot and killed a porcupine. His father hunted animals for food, but he did not kill them for sport. Angry, he ordered the two boys to skin and cook and eat the porcupine. Harold said later, "We cooked the haunches for hours, but they were still about as tender and tasty as a piece of shoe leather."[49]

• When Rain Pryor, one of Richard Pryor's daughters, prepared to celebrate her 16th birthday, she thought that it would be fun to have an all-girl party, but she changed her mind when the guests began to arrive. She told her mother, Shelley, "I wish I'd invited the guys." Her mother reminded her that she had been the one who had invited only girls. "I know," Rain admitted, "but it seems silly now." After a while, however, someone played Cyndi Lauper's "Girls Just Want to Have Fun," and three boys — dressed in drag — joined the party. The three boys were Rain's best male friends — her mother had called them and invited them to the "all-girl" party. Rain's maternal grandmother was feisty. She was a good cook, and she shared her recipes with other people. However, she admitted, "But sometimes, if they're not so nice, I leave out a key ingredient." Her father, of course, had a good sense of humor. When a very young Rain brought a boy over to meet her father, Mr. Pryor met the boy while holding a shotgun. He asked the boy, "What are your intentions with my daughter, young man?"[50]

• Moe Howard of Three Stooges fame had long, lovely curls when he was a child, with the result that he fought a lot of kids who teased him about his curls after he started attending school. When he entered kindergarten, a kind teacher, Mrs. Warner, seated him near a girl with even longer curls than his own so that his curls would not be so noticeable. She also tried — without success — to get his mother to give him a regular boy's haircut. Eventually, Moe got tired of fighting and instead took the verbal abuse. He did make a friend of a new boy in the neighborhood whose name was Donald McMann, who stood up for him when a bully taunted him about his curls. Don knocked the bully out with one punch, and after the bully regained consciousness, Don forced him to apologize to Moe in front of several children who had watched the bullying. Finally, Moe himself cut off his long curls, resulting in the bowl-shaped haircut that he later made famous all over the world. When his mother saw his new haircut, she told him, "Thank God you did it. I didn't have the courage."[51]

• When cartoon creator Chuck Jones was a little boy, he discovered a magic gumball machine that dispensed a gumball even when a little boy did not put a penny in it. Soon, little Chuck had dozens of gumballs — so many that they would not all fit in his overflowing pockets. An inventive boy, he discovered that by tying his pants legs tight at the knee, he could put more gumballs down his pants and carry them home that way. At home, he stored all the gumballs in a small chest under his bed. The palms of his hands were multi-colored from the dye of the gumballs, but he kept them hidden from his parents as he ate. Unfortunately, as he was undressing that night for bed, his mother came into his room and saw his knees, which were also multi-colored. She called in his father to look at their son's knees. Fortunately, his father laughed and said that young Chuck had improved his knees' appearance. Young Chuck was able to keep the secret of his multi-colored knees from his mother by bribing his brother and sisters with gumballs.[52]

• George Burns and Gracie Allen adopted two children: a boy and a girl. One evening, while their friends Harpo and Susan Marx were visiting, the telephone rang with news that a four-week-old girl was available for adoption. Gracie explained that their family was already complete, and Harpo rushed to the telephone, took it, and said that he was willing to adopt the girl. The next day, he was on the train to make all the necessary arrangements for the adoption. George asked Harpo how many children he and Susan wanted; after all, they had already adopted three children before adopting this four-week-old girl. Harpo replied, "We want to adopt one child for every window we have in the house so that when we leave, we can look back and see one of our kids in every window waving to us."[53]

• Anne Fine, author of *Alias Madame Doubtfire*, has a daughter who can quickly make up her mind. At dinner one day, the daughter frowned at something that was on her plate and asked, "What is this?" Hearing the answer, she asked, "*Duck* duck? You mean, like on the pond?" Ms. Fine admitted the fact, and her daughter pushed away her plate and became a vegetarian.[54]

• Before an outing with her four-year-old grandson, Creators Syndicate columnist Connie Schultz made the kind of preparations that many women make. As she put on blush, her grandson asked, "Grandma, what are you doing?" She replied, "I'm putting on my makeup, honey. It makes me look better." After a few seconds had gone by, he asked, "When does it start working?"[55]

**Celebrities**

• Ray Bradbury has met many celebrities in his long life, including from before he became famous. Growing up in Los Angeles helped. In October 1938, when he was 18 years old, he walked by the Biltmore, where a performance of George Bernard Shaw's *Candida* was playing. Suddenly, someone ran out of the theater and ran into him. She looked at him, and he looked at her. Then she took off running again. The woman was Greta Garbo. He knew the theater's ticket-taker, and she explained to him that the theater frequently sold Ms. Garbo a seat in the back row. Ms. Garbo arrived after the theater was dark, and as soon as the play was over, she took off running out of the theater. And in February 1935, at the Academy Awards during a time when police did not show up to control the crowd, Ray saw Bette Davis trying unsuccessfully to open a side door into the Biltmore for the award ceremony. Ray opened the door for her, and she went inside. Ray says, "I helped Bette Davis to get in to win her first Academy Award." She won the Best Actress Oscar in 1935 for *Dangerous* and in 1938 for *Jezebel*.[56]

• In 1957, Gypsy Rose Lee, a stripper in burlesque, wrote a sensational autobiography titled *Gypsy*, which many people of wit and intelligence have admired. A woman of wit and intelligence herself, Ms. Lee once told the police after a police raid, "I wasn't naked. I was completely covered by a blue spotlight." Very likely, she wasn't naked. She often wore a flesh-colored bodysuit underneath the clothing she took off. Critic Carl Rollyson once wrote, "With wit and sass, Gypsy Rose Lee transformed herself from a burlesque dancer into a nationwide celebrity. She also wrote her own life story, a masterpiece her biographers still struggle to match."[57]

**Christmas**

• Young people's author Jon Scieszka used to get bad birthday presents because his birthday was about the time that he had to go back to school after summer vacation. His presents were things like socks and stuff that he would need for school. But he admits that he and his five brothers gave even worse presents to their parents. For example, their father's birthday was on Christmas Eve, so on his birthday they would give him a salt shaker and on Christmas they would give him a pepper shaker. Or they would give him one cuff link on Christmas Eve and the other cuff link on Christmas. Their mother's birthday was in the summer, and they would buy for her the shiniest necklace or bracelet they could get for $1.50 at the drugstore. Funny thing, though: Although she always seemed appreciative to get jewelry from her boys on her birthday, she never seemed to actually wear the jewelry. And she never actually used the $1.50 perfume they sometimes bought her. One day, Jon and his brother Jim noticed a glow-in-the-dark Frisbee in the drugstore. Jim said, "This is amazing." Jon said, "We could really use one of those." Jim said, "Let's get it for Mom." And so the boys started to get their mother things that they wanted. This was a win-win situation. The boys got to play with their gifts to their mother, and their mother was secretly relieved not to get gifts of $1.50 jewelry and $1.50 perfume.[58]

• Jimmy Durante's most memorable Christmas was in the year 1961. That is when he and his wife, Margie, adopted a baby girl named Cecilia. Of course, as babies do, this baby cried. And every time the baby cried, Mr. and Mrs. Durante were panic-stricken and called the doctor. The baby periodically cried all night long, and Mr. and Mrs. Durante periodically called the doctor all night long. Mr. Durante says, "I'll bet that was the doctor's most memorable Christmas, too."[59]

**Comedians**

• One of the people Roy Clark worked with on *Hee Haw* was Junior Samples, who was a country boy who made his own moonshine — for real. Junior became famous without trying to. His brother had caught a big sea bass in the Gulf of Mexico and brought its head back home to Georgia. Junior showed the head of the sea bass to people, but he told them that he had caught it right there in Georgia in a fresh-water lake. People marveled at the size of the fish head and thought that it must have been the biggest fish ever caught in Georgia. Junior even went on a radio show and talked about the fish. Country comedian Archie Campbell heard a tape of the radio show, liked what he heard, wrote a script based on Junior's story, and hunted up Junior and made a recording that became a country comedy hit. The producers who were creating *Hee Haw* heard about Junior, liked what they heard, and signed him up to be on TV. Shortly after joining the *Hee Haw* cast, Junior asked Roy, whom he had seen often on TV, how he had come to be on *Hee Haw*. Roy told his story of a long apprenticeship in music and many years of experience entertaining people. Junior said, "Huh! I just told a lie about a fish, and here I am!" On *Hee Haw* and in real life, Junior always wore bib overalls, a tee shirt, and a baseball cap. Back in the days when Spiro Agnew was Vice President of the United States, Junior was invited to a fancy party in a penthouse in Nashville, Tennessee. For such a fancy party, Junior was expected to dress properly and he was given a tuxedo jacket — which he wore over his bib overalls and tee shirt. At the party, he was introduced to the Vice President of CBS, and as you may expect, he said, "Nice to meet you, Mr. Sparyou Agnew."[60]

• For over 50 years, Max Patkin was the Clown Prince of Baseball. He had a rubbery body that sometimes seemed to move of its own volition, and on his oversized uniform he wore a question mark instead of a number. Among other talents, he could act like a human geyser, spewing a stream of water six feet into the air. At a minor-league doubleheader in 1967 at which Mad Max was to perform, umpire John McSherry and his partner ran into some bother. His umpire partner threw out the home-team catcher, and then threw out the home-team manager, both in the first game. Before the second game, the home-team manager was still so angry that he refused to come out of the dugout and give the umpires his lineup card. This time, it was Umpire McSherry who threw the home-team manager out of the game, telling him, "Don't bother to come out with the lineup cards 'cause you're gone again." The manager came out of the dugout with the lineup cards, but Umpire McSherry told him, "I can't take those from you because you're not here." This led to a 45-minute disagreement between the manager and the umpires, with the umpires winning, of course — they even threw the home-team catcher out of the game again. At that time, Mad Max came out to do his act, and as he passed the umpires, he complained, "How am I gonna follow you two guys?"[61]

• Comedian Red Skelton was robbed and burgled a few times in his life. Once, in Las Vegas, a man with a gun demanded all his cash. Red handed over the couple of hundred dollars he was carrying, but the man with the gun recognized him and said, "I wouldn't rob you, Mr. Skelton." Red told him to keep the money: "You must need it, young man, or you wouldn't have gone through all this trouble." Red, who spent the early part of his career impoverished, did spend a lot of money during his life, but sometimes he did not part with money easily. He once saw a painting he liked and asked the art dealer how much it cost. The art dealer snootily replied, "Five thousand wouldn't take that." Red left, saying, "I'm one of the five thousand."[62]

• The Reverend Warren Debenham, a San Francisco-area minister, collects comedy records — many thousands of them. He says that good comedy "puts down the people in power, whereas bad comedy puts down the guy who's powerless. For that reason, I really don't like Andrew Dice Clay: He puts down women and gays." The reverend also says that many religious people have hobbies outside of their ministry. For example, he knows a clergyman who is an expert on photographing wildflowers. Reverend Debenham says that this clergyman will "fiddle for hours just getting the right light and focus. [The clergyman] said, 'That's how I get the urge to manipulate *out* of my system — so I don't manipulate *people*.'"[63]

- During his act one night, comedian Sam Kinison got violent and bashed a hole in a wall. Of course, the owner of the club wouldn't let him do his act any longer and suspended him for a couple of weeks. In response, Mr. Kinison protested by driving to the club and acting out a mock crucifixion. He stripped himself almost naked (wearing only a towel), poured ketchup all over himself, and tied himself in crucifixion position to a sign, all while shouting, "Help! They're crucifying me! They're crucifying my talent across the street." This got him a lot of publicity, and after the two weeks of his suspension were up, he had a huge crowd waiting to see him back at the club.[64]
- British comedian Hugh Dennis remembers the most embarrassing moment of his life. It was when he had a colonoscopy: "The nurse was just about to insert 50 feet of hosepipe into the most embarrassing part of my anatomy. Just as I was dropping off, the nurse said, 'I'm a very good friend of your next-door neighbor.'" Mr. Dennis says that he does not have a most valued possession for a very good reason: "I'd rather have nothing worth stealing than live my life trying to protect things."[65]
- Fame is not always pleasant. Gracie Allen, part of a famous comedy team with her husband, George Burns, once went into Bloomingdale's to buy a rolling pin. The saleswoman waiting on her said to her, "I suppose that's to hit George with," and started laughing at her own joke. Soon, lots of people were around Gracie and laughing. Gracie said, "I got so embarrassed I dropped the rolling pin and bought two end tables instead."[66]
- Before becoming famous on TV, David Letterman had some miserable times as a stand-up comedian. Once, in Lake Tahoe, his 25-minute stand-up routine was over in 15 minutes because the audience did not laugh at his jokes. He points out, "You take the laughs out of your act and the time really flies." Also in Lake Tahoe, someone asked him if he was Dave Etterman — the L had fallen off the sign outside.[67]

- Don Rickles knows the world's best punch line; unfortunately, he is not the person who said it. A homeless man once asked him, "Got any spare change?" Mr. Rickles gave him $5 and said, "Go buy yourself a ranch." The homeless man thanked him and started to walk away, then turned around and said, "Now I need cattle."[68]

**Critics**

- David Thomson's often revised *The New Biographical Dictionary of Film* is the kind of book that readers love to argue with. In it, Mr. Thomson writes brief essays about important figures in film. Readers can argue with Mr. Thomson's opinions, and they can argue that people who have been left out ought to be included and perhaps that people who are in the book ought not to be in it. One person who loved to argue with the book (and who recognizes Mr. Thomson's strengths as well as his supposed weaknesses) was the critic Clive James. He also had fun pointing out an amusing error in the book that illustrates the difficulty of revising a large book. In a review, Mr. James writes, "The entry for Teresa Wright starts with the information that she died in 2005 and ends with the observation: 'She has not done too much lately ...' And that would be because?"[69]

- Glasgow poet George Outram heard a friend praise a preacher whom he felt ought not to be praised, so he composed these lines: "I cannot praise the Doctor's eyes, / I never saw his glance divine; / He always shuts them when he prays, / And when he preaches he shuts mine."[70]

**Death**

- The Mizners lived at a time when many great American bankers were Jewish. In 1906, a massively destructive earthquake rocked San Francisco and Lansing Mizner headed a delegation that went to New York to borrow money with which to rebuild the city. At one New York banquet at which many after-dinner speeches were given, Lansing was asked to make a speech on the qualities that made for a great banker. Lansing's speech was very short: "Circumcision." He got a big laugh, and San Francisco borrowed big money. When Lansing died, his brother, Addison, informed another brother, Wilson, a Hollywood screenwriter, while he was dressing. The Mizners loved each other, but they refused to be made fools of by fate and they met misfortune with fortitude and humor. Wilson said to Addison, "I wish you'd told me before I put on this red necktie."[71]

• At one time, the Everglades Club in Palm Beach excluded Jews. Some friends invited Jewish atheist Christopher Hitchens and his wife, Carol Blue, to dine there. When the waiter arrived, Mr. Hitchens, known for confronting stupidity throughout his life, asked, "Do you have a kosher menu?" Mr. Hitchens once heard about a professor who would seduce the female students in his creative-writing seminars. Mr. Hitchens said, "It's not worth it. Afterward, you have to read their short stories." He died of cancer, and he enjoyed gallows humor. When a nurse asked him how he was feeling, he used to reply, "I seem to have a little touch of cancer."[72]

• Early in her adult life, Ruth Rendell, who also writes using the pen name Barbara Vine, had a job as a reporter for the *Chigwell Times*. She was fired after she wrote an article about a local tennis club's dinner without actually attending the dinner — and therefore did not know that the speaker had died while giving his speech. As an author, she wrote often about death and murderers, but she said, "I've never met a murderer as far as I know. I would hate to. It's just not necessary." By the way, she married Don Rendell, her former boss at the *Chigwell Times*.[73]

• To a junkie, drugs are more important than everything else. Mason Hoffenberg, who co-wrote *Candy* with Terry Southern, was addicted to heroin and other illegal drugs for many years. In London, England, in the 1960s, where and when prescriptions for heroin were still legal, he showed up at a doctor's office only to be told by a white-faced nurse that the doctor had just died of a heart attack. Mr.

Hoffenberg replied, "Yeah, whatever, but what about my prescription?"[74]

• English novelist Anthony Trollope once heard a couple of clergymen complaining about a character who appeared frequently in his novels: Mrs. Proudie, whom they found annoying. Mr. Trollope introduced himself to the two clergymen, and he promised, "I will go home and kill her before the week is over." He then wrote her death scene in his newest novel.[75]

**Education**

• Stephen King started writing early. When he was in the seventh grade, he wrote an eight-page adaptation of the movie *The Pit and the Pendulum*, which was very loosely based on the Edgar Allen Poe short story. Stephen made about 40 copies of his adaptation and sold every copy for 25 cents. Unfortunately for Stephen, the school principal made him give the money back and told him not to sell "junk like this" at the school. When Stephen was in high school, he created the underground publication *The Village Vomit*, which made fun of teachers. School officials made him apologize to the most offended teacher and also got him a job as a sports writer on the local weekly newspaper.

Mr. King's first published book was *Carrie*, for which he got an advance of $2,500. When the paperback rights for the novel sold for $400,000, of which Mr. King got half (his publishing company got the other half), he wanted to celebrate with his wife, but she was not home. He walked across the street and into a drugstore and bought her the best gift he could find: a hair dryer.

Because Mr. King has written much genre fiction, many people do not give him credit as a serious writer. An elderly woman once saw him and said, "I know who you are! You're that horror writer. You're Stephen King." He admitted the fact, and she told him, "I don't read what you do. I respect what you do, but I don't read it. Why don't you write something uplifting sometime, like that *Shawshank Redemption*?"

He said, "I did write that." She told him, "No, you didn't." (Mr. King did write the novella *Rita Hayworth and Shawshank Redemption*, upon which the movie *The Shawshank Redemption* is based.)[76]

- Teller of Penn and Teller fame was greatly influenced by a high-school teacher named D.G. Rosenbaum, who was also an actor and a magician. He wore pince-nez and a black goatee, and he smoked black cigarettes. On a snowy day that forced many students to miss school, he read a 1916 short story by Max Beerbohm titled "Enoch Soames" in which the title character, a man with a big ego, made a deal with the devil in which he exchanged his soul for a magical trip to the future — 2:10 P.M. on 3 June 1997 in the Round Reading Room at the British Museum — so he could look at the shelves of books that would have by then been written about him. Unfortunately, he discovers that he has been forgotten. The only place his name appears in the library is in a short story by Max Beerbohm. Teller flew to England and at 2:10 P.M. on 3 June 1997 he was in Round Reading Room at the British Museum along with about a dozen people who had been impressed by the short story. In fact, a man did appear out of the stacks and did ask about Enoch Soames and why there were no volumes about him on the shelves before he disappeared back into the stacks. One of the people in the Round Reading Room said, "I'm having to fight tears." Did Teller hire an actor? He said, "Taking credit for it that day would be a terrible thing — a terrible, terrible thing. That's answering the question that you must not answer."[77]

- Philosopher Simon Critchley studied undergraduate philosophy under Frank Cioffi, who taught for a while in Singapore, where his office was infested with large cockroaches. Professor Cioffi put out poison for the cockroaches, and he watched a cockroach die in agony after eating some of the poison. Professor Cioffi told Simon what he learned from the experience: "There is a problem with other minds after all. It is a real issue. I knew that the bug was dying in pain and felt profound sympathy and stopped doing it."

Simon once asked him for permission to change courses. "Which courses?" he asked. "I'm meant to be reading Foucault, but I want to do a course on Derrida." "Man," he replied, "that's like going from horseshit to bullshit." Mr. Critchley notes that "bullshit" was a favorite word of Professor Cioffi and that Professor Cioffi's approach to philosophy was this: "No BS."

One more story: Professor Cioffi was in a hospital, and a friend who wanted to visit him asked a nurse where was Professor Cioffi. The nurse said, "Oh, you mean the patient who knows all the answers." Professor Cioffi was close enough to hear, and he said, "No, I know all the questions."[78]

• Nathaniel Hawthorne, author of *The House of Seven Gables*, was a little wild while he was attending Bowdoin College. He played cards and gambled, drank alcohol and smoked tobacco, and cut class — all of which were against the rules of the college. In May 1822, William Allen, the president of Bowdoin, sent his mother a letter that said in part: "By the vote of the executive government of this college, it is made my duty to request your cooperation with us in the attempt to induce your son faithfully to observe the laws of this institution." After he was caught gambling, the college fined him 50 cents. At the time, that amount of money would buy enough food to feed a person for two days. He wrote his mother and asked her to pay the fine. He also promised not to gamble again — at least until the last week of the term. In May of his senior year, he received a bill. The cost of his tuition was $2, and the cost of his fines was $2.36. The college fined him 20 cents for not turning in papers, 20 cents for missing church, 36 cents for missing prayers, and $1.60 for cutting class.[79]

• Mary Bly is a Renaissance scholar at Fordham University, and Eloisa James is a best-selling romance novelist. They are the same person. Ms. Bly for a long time kept secret the fact that she wrote romance novels using a pseudonym, worried that it could hurt her chances at gaining tenure. But once she earned tenure, she came out of the romance closet. In February 2011 she passed out copies of her romances following the end of a faculty meeting. The back cover photographs showed the author: Eloisa James, who is Ms. Bly without eyeglasses. Professional colleague Eva Badowska said, "I was speechless." Ms. Bly began reading romance novels as a young adult. She said, "I learned a lot about sex from those books. I remember sitting on the school bus going, How? Where?" Her father, poet Robert Bly, was OK with her reading romance novels, but the two did have an agreement: she had to read one classic novel for every five romance novels she read.[80]

• Nora Ephron started her career as a journalist, although she is now best known for writing the screenplays to such movies as *Silkwood*, *Sleepless in Seattle*, and *When Harry Met Sally*. In high school, her journalism teacher taught her an important lesson. The students sat in front of the manual typewriters that journalists used back then, and the teacher gave them the information they needed to write their first assignment: a story about all the faculty traveling to Sacramento, California, next Thursday for a colloquium on teaching methods. The students typed their stories, the teacher scanned the students' leads, and then the teacher announced, "The lead to the story is, '*There will be no school next Thursday*.'" Ms. Ephron says, "It was a breathtaking moment. In that instant I realized that journalism was not just about regurgitating the facts but about figuring out the point. It wasn't enough to know the who, what, when, and where; you had to understand what it meant. And why it mattered."[81]

• Growing up with a cartoon creator for your father can have disadvantages. Chuck Jones directed and co-wrote the cartoon "For Scent-imental Reasons," starring amorous skunk Pepé le Pew. His daughter, Linda, saw the cartoon just before she entered a junior high school spelling bee. She was asked to spell the word "sentimental." Guess how she spelled it? Chuck remembered, "She came home furious." When Linda was little and she and her friends were watching a Bugs Bunny cartoon, she told her friends that her father had drawn the cartoon — which he had. Unfortunately, they did not believe her. One child even said, "Yeah, sure, and *my* father's Clark Gable." Given the time and place the Jones family was living, that may even have been true. And when Linda was four years old, she drank a teaspoonful of champagne and sugar to celebrate New Year's Eve. Asked if she liked it, she said, "Yes, it's full of jokes."[82]

• During the mid-1980s, art historian Michael Fried and literary theorist Stanley Fish taught together at the Johns Hopkins University a course on interpretation to 40 undergraduates. One day, half the class was absent. Mr. Fish told the 20 students who had shown up, "It has just come to the attention of Professor Fried and me that today's attendance is impermissibly down. We are going to step out for a cup of coffee and will come back at 11 for the second hour of class. You will do this: Find every absent student in this class and all of you ... will ... be ... here when we return." The two teachers left the classroom and went to a cafeteria, where Mr. Fried asked Mr. Fish, "Stanley, what happens if we get back and it hasn't worked? What do we do?" Mr. Fish replied, "I have no idea." (Within the hour, every student was in the classroom.)[83]

• When comedian Paul Mooney was in a science class in high school, he was talking in class about something that was not science, so his teacher told him, "This is science class. We don't discuss that here, so be quiet." Mr. Mooney kept quiet for three months. After three months, his teacher asked him to shut the back door. Mr. Mooney replied, "This is a science class, not a domestics class, and you can shut your own door." This got a big laugh from the students, not so much because of what he had said, but because he had waited three months to say it. His teacher was cool about it, by the way, merely saying, "Touché."[84]

• While Joseph Harris was in graduate school, he wrote a paper in which he concentrated on rebutting as forcibly as possible the views of a certain scholar. His professor read the paper and then asked him, "Why are you spending so much time discussing the work of someone you seem to think isn't very bright?" Since then, he has tried to resist the temptation to write essays that merely show that someone else is wrong.[85]

• Isaac Asimov believed in the importance of lifelong learning. He told a story about nonagenarian Oliver Wendell Holmes Jr. studying a Greek grammar while he was in a hospital. Visitor Theodore Roosevelt pointed out Mr. Holmes was well into his 90s and asked him why he was reading a Greek grammar. Mr. Holmes replied, "To improve my mind, Mr. President."[86]

• Sidney Morgenbesser, who taught philosophy at Columbia, was once described as a "mind on the loose." The philosopher Robert Nozick spent his undergraduate years at Columbia and said that he "majored in Sidney Morgenbesser." On his deathbed, Morgenbesser asked, "Why is God making me suffer so much? Just because I don't believe in him?"[87]

• Comedian Fred Allen was funny even when he was still in school. While standing in front of a class and demonstrating an algebra problem, he said, "Let X stand for my father's signature."[88]

**Fans**

• Ray Bradbury was a fan of Walt Disney ever since the early days of Mickey Mouse. Seeing him carrying a big load of Christmas presents on Saks Avenue, Ray introduced himself to Walt, who of course knew who he was. Ray said, "Someday, soon, I'd like to take you to lunch." Walt delighted him by saying, "Tomorrow." At the lunch, Ray said to Walt, "I wish you would run for mayor." Walt replied, "Ray, why should I be mayor when I'm already king?"

When Ray visited Disneyland for the first time, he went with his friend Charles Laughton, a great actor who had played Captain Bligh in the classic movie *Mutiny on the Bounty*. While on the Jungle Ride,

Mr. Laughton had fun pretending to be a comedic Captain Bligh who keelhauled pirates and gave orders.

Ray liked Walt and wrote articles defending him against critics. When Ray visited him again, Walt asked, "Ray, you've done so much for us. What can *we* do for *you*?" Ray replied, "Walt, open the vaults!" Walt made a phone call and ordered, "Open the vaults. I'm sending Ray over. He can have anything he wants." Ray left with an armload of cels that had been used to make *Snow White*, *Sleeping Beauty*, and *Alice in Wonderland*. Ray wrote later, "I felt guilty, but elated. I couldn't stop stacking."

After Walt's death, Ray wrote, "Walt left the world a thousand times better than when he arrived. He personified [Albert] Schweitzer's quote, 'Do something good. Someone may imitate it.'"[89]

• Comedian Jonathan Winters sometimes had to deal with negative people — which provided an outlet for his fertile brain. Someone once asked him, "Aren't you somewhat of a has-been?" He replied, "No question about it, but I'm an international has-been whereas you're just a local has-been." Mr. Winters once created a bitter epitaph for his gravestone: "Step on me. Everyone else did." Of course, not everything in his life was bitter. Robin Williams and many other comedians were fans of his. The Ohio-born Mr. Winters once told Mr. Williams to stop referring to him as a mentor: "That's a bad word in Ohio. Say 'idol.'"[90]

• A police officer stopped a speeding Chico Marx, recognized him, and told him that his children were big fans. Chico offered to send them some autographed photographs, but the police officer replied, "Better not — my wife can't stand you."[91]

**Fathers**

• The father of author Ben Okri, winner of the Booker Prize for Fiction in 1991 for *The Famished Road*, was educated in law in London. While there, he amassed a collection of the great classics of literature, including Homer, Shakespeare, Dickens, Dostoevsky, and Tolstoy, and took them with him and his family to Nigeria. There he became very busy as a lawyer and had no time to read the classic books, which gathered dust. Once in a while, he would tell his son, "Ben, dust the books — but don't read them!" Ben says, "That made the books fantastically attractive. I don't know if he did it on purpose. I wouldn't put it past him." Anyway, Ben would read for hours, until his father would ask, "Ben, what are you doing?" Then Ben would begin to dust the books again. Today, Ben says, "Books still have this tension for me — the do and don't, the possibility of danger, of secret knowledge. It makes them very potent."[92]

• Jay Leno's father sold insurance in Harlem, a district to which he had requested that he be assigned. The policies cost a nickel a week, and each week Jay's father went into Harlem and collected nickels. After his father died, Jay talked about him on TV. Afterward, he received a letter from an African-American woman who remembered a white man named Angelo who came into Harlem each week and collected nickels. The white man always had a lollipop for her, and he was the only white man who had ever eaten dinner with her family in their house. Jay telephoned her and said that yes, that man was his father. Jay says, "Her whole attitude toward white people was based on that one nice white man she met in her childhood, who always treated her with kindness and respect, and always gave her a piece of candy and asked her what she wanted to be when she grew up."[93]

• Comedian Joey Bishop used to play golf at Englewood Country Club, where his caddy was Grumpy, so-called because he looked like one of the Disney dwarfs in *Snow White and the Seven Dwarfs*. Mr. Bishop was playing at the Copacabana, and Grumpy, who had been drinking and had sold or hocked his false teeth, wanted to see the show, so he told Jules Podell, who ran the nightclub, that he was Mr. Bishop's father — a major lie. Mr. Podell gave Grumpy the best table in the nightclub. After the show, Mr. Podell said to Mr. Bishop, "What's the matter, you bum — I don't pay you enough that you can buy your father some teeth?"[94]

• Henry Taylor, a poet who won the Pulitzer Prize in 1986, rode horses in competitions when he was growing up. While Henry was waiting to compete in the Junior FEI class, someone asked his father if he wanted to see the horse that was going to win the Junior FEI class. Loyal to his son, his father simply looked in the van at Henry's horse and said, "I don't need to move. I can see her just fine from here." In fact, Henry and his horse won.[95]

• Swedish author Stieg Larsson became internationally famous with the publication of the crime series *Millennium Trilogy*, of which the title of the first volume was translated as *The Girl with the Dragon Tattoo*. For his 13th birthday, his father bought an expensive typewriter for him after reading a novel that Stieg had written in a notebook. In addition to being expensive, the typewriter was noisy. Stieg's father says that "we had to make space for him in the cellar. He would write in the cellar and come up for meals, but at least we could sleep at night."[96]

**Feminism**

• The Egyptian writer Nawal Elsaadawi was both a novelist and a feminist. She also wrote volumes of autobiography. In *A Daughter of Isis*, she recalled learning that boys were valued much more than girls. Her grandmother told her that "a boy is worth 15 girls at least [...]. Girls are a blight." Nawal was angry and stamped her foot.

Also in *A Daughter of Isis*, she wrote about being circumcised: "When I was six, the *daya* [midwife] came along holding a razor, pulled out my clitoris from between my thighs and cut it off. She said it was the will of God and she had done his will [...]. I lay in a pool of blood. After a few days the bleeding stopped [...]. But the pain was there like an abscess deep in my flesh [...]. I did not know what other parts in my body there were that might need to be cut off in the same way." She campaigned against female circumcision for 50 years, and in 2008 it was banned, but it still occurs in Egypt.

She also was expected to be a child bride: "When I was a child, it was normal that girls in my village would marry at 10 or 11." However, she resisted by blackening her teeth and spilling coffee on a would-be bridegroom. She married a few times, and in *Walking Through Fire*, another volume of autobiography, she wrote about how a lawyer to whom she was married refused to grant her a divorce, saying, "It is the man who decides to divorce and not the woman." She threatened him with a scalpel, and he decided to get a divorce, something he should have agreed to earlier. After all, he had given her an ultimatum: She had to choose between him and her writing. She chose her writing.[97]

**Fights**
- Walt Whitman was a loafer — and proud of it. According to Mr. Whitman, "Of all human beings, none equals your genuine, inborn, unvarying loafer. What was Adam, I should like to know, but a loafer?" Mr. Whitman was rumored to have left one job because he had become so angry that he had kicked a politician down some stairs, but people who knew him disagreed with this: "Whoever knows him well will laugh at the idea of his *kicking any body*, much less a prominent politician. He is too indolent [lazy] to kick a musketo [mosquito]." He declined to work on his family's farm, preferring instead to go to the beach. He said, "I was a first-rate aquatic loafer. I possessed almost unlimited capacity for floating on my back."[98]
- Heywood Broun was on a voyage once when he was asked — for the sake of entertaining his fellow passengers — to fight another man of approximately his own weight and stature. He agreed, but when he met the man he was supposed to fight, the man said to Mr. Broun, "I'm going to ask you a question which I have wanted to ask someone ever since I got on this ship. What is this 'demitasse' they have on the bill of fare?" Mr. Broun immediately canceled the fight, saying, "Any chap who doesn't know what a 'demitasse' is must be a tough guy."[99]

# Chapter 3: From Food to Language

**Food**

- M.F.K. Fisher wrote about food, but she denied that she was a food writer. Of course, she was an authority on food, and that led to a problem. She explained that she received many fan letters, including some from celebrities, but the letters tend to end, "We'd love to have you come to dinner, but we wouldn't dare ask you." This means, Ms. Fisher said, "They don't. And I eat a lovely rye crisp at home."

Ms. Fisher was good company, even if her companions sometimes weren't. She lived in France for a few years, and she acquired a French friend who wished to be helpful and who thought that Ms. Fisher knew much less than she knew. The result? Ms. Fisher said, "She explained to me things that I had known for decades."

As a food expert, she knew good food, and she avoided bad food. Once, she was out with her daughter and granddaughter. They were hungry, so they stopped at a McDonald's and each got a hamburger. Each took a bite or two of her hamburger and decided that actually they were not all that hungry. Driving home, Ms. Fisher thought that something was wrong with her car because it smelled funny. She remembers, "When we got home, I said to my daughter, 'Don't you want me to warm up your hamburger? You must be hungry.' I warmed it up, and then I knew why the car smelled funny." The hamburgers ended up in the garbage pail.

According to Ms. Fisher, it is wise to eat fast food quickly or it will decompose into its original ingredient. When someone asked her what fast food's original ingredient is, she replied, "Bilgewater."

It is possible, of course, that Ms. Fisher's children have well-developed taste buds. When her older daughter, Anne, was an infant, Ms. Fisher fed her a spoonful of Gerber's strained beans. Ms. Fisher remembers that Anne looked at her as if to ask, "Why are you doing this to me?" Ms. Fisher never gave her Gerber's baby food again.[100]

• In one of comedian Red Skelton's funniest routines, he demonstrated the way that different kinds of people eat doughnuts. Each time he performed the sketch, he ate nine doughnuts. In vaudeville, he did five shows a day, eating 45 doughnuts a day, which means that he ate 315 doughnuts each week! Once he gained 35 pounds doing the routine, and he was forced to stop performing it so that he could lose some weight.

Mr. Skelton was a funny man, but he could get his comedy writers angry at him. When he was doing his weekly comedy TV series, a reporter asked him what the source of inspiration for his comedy sketches was. Mr. Skelton raised his eyes toward heaven and replied, "God." His comedy writers preferred that they be given some of the credit, so they presented him with some blank pages and this note: "Please have God fill in the empty pages."[101]

• The late poet Benjamin Zephaniah was a vegan, and he had interesting experiences with food. When he was a young man, he was in prison, and he served food; however, prison officials made him serve specially prepared food to sex offenders and members of the Irish Republican Army. He says that "the prison officers made me put custard on their main courses and gravy on their puddings."

In his poem "Vegan Delight," which contains the words "Ackees, chapattis, dumplins an' naan, channa and rotis, onion uttapam," he answers a question that people commonly ask him: What does he, a vegan, eat? When he moved to a small village in Lincolnshire, his neighbors surprised him by leaving gifts of vegetables and fruits from their gardens and orchards outside his door. Although he was born in England, his background is Jamaican, and he says about the gifts, "At first I thought it was some kind of witchcraft."[102]

• Before Patti Smith became famous, she took exactly 55 cents to an Automat to buy a cheese-and-lettuce sandwich, but after she had deposited the coins, the window would not open. Disappointed, she noticed that the price had gone up to 65 cents. Suddenly, a voice behind her said, "Can I help?" She turned around and saw poet Allen Ginsberg, who gave her the dime she needed to buy the sandwich. They talked together, and suddenly he asked her, "Are you a girl?" She replied, "Yeah. Is that a problem?" He said, "I'm sorry. I took you for a very pretty boy." Patti writes, "I got the picture immediately." She then asked him, "Well, does this mean I return the sandwich?" Fortunately, Allen said, "No, enjoy it. It was my mistake."[103]

• Syndicated columnist Marc Dion took a long time to get married, so in his bachelor days much of his food was such things as baloney sandwiches and canned spaghetti. At work, he heard that olive oil was good for you and so each morning he would pour olive oil into a shot glass and drink it. When he told a woman at work what he was doing, she was shocked and told him that he was supposed to cook with the olive oil. She also told him something else that he told his 75-year-old mother: "One of the women at work said she didn't know how I could drink a shot glass of olive oil without throwing up." His mother replied, "You tell her my son can drink ANYTHING if it's in a shot glass."[104]

• Musician Quincy Jones once had lunch — sole meunière — with his then-neighbor Pablo Picasso at Cannes, France. Mr. Picasso had an interesting way of paying for his meal. Mr. Jones remembers, "When he finished, he took his plate on to the Croisette so the sun could parch the bones. He took out his colors — red, yellow, and blue — and drew his designs on the plate beside the fish bones. And when the waiter brought *l'addition* [the bill], he gave him the plate. And there were Picasso's plates all around the wall. That's how he paid for his dinners."[105]

**Friends**

• Playwright Robert Sherwood was very tall. (He was six-foot-seven in an era before seven footers became common in the NBA.) Once humorist Robert Benchley was asked if he knew Mr.

Sherwood. Mr. Benchley stood on a chair, raised his hand in the air, and said, "Why, I've known Bob Sherwood since he was *this* high."[106]
- Author Michael Thomas Ford has a friend named Gretchen who is a professor of philosophy. When people ask her what she does for fun, she replies, "I like to think."[107]

**Gambling**
- Heywood Broun enjoyed gambling, but after he had been losing too much at the roulette wheel, his second wife, Connie, suggested that he not play it for at least a few days. Heywood, however, did not want to stop playing. Running into his friend Frank Sullivan, he discovered that Frank had a slight cold. That evening, he told Connie that Frank had very bad laryngitis and asked, "Don't you think I ought to go over and see Frank and see how he is?" As you would expect, Connie said, "Of course, by all means do that." And Heywood went gambling. The next night much the same thing happened, although Frank, a professional humorist, says that Heywood gave him "about a dozen more diseases" and "If I had had all the diseases that Heywood thought up for me on those two nights, the Harvard Medical Museum would have been bidding on me." Unfortunately for Heywood, Connie ran into Frank, who seemed to her to be perfectly healthy, and Heywood's gambling and Frank's illnesses came to an end.[108]
- Bob Hope and Bing Crosby went to the race track and engaged in a contest to see who could pick the most winners. Each of them gambled on each race at the betting window, and each of them picked the winner in each race! Bing knew that Bob did not know a lot about horses, so he asked him how he had managed to pick all the winners. Bob confessed that he had bet on *every* horse in each race. Bing then said, "I thought you'd do something like that, so in order not to be outsmarted, I did the same thing."[109]
- George Burns remembers a day when Jimmy Durante and Eddie Cantor could do no wrong at the Del Mar racetrack. A horse owner gave them a tip on the race, and they won, betting $100 on a 20-to-1

horse. And they had winning tickets for the next five races. Mr. Durante then said to Mr. Cantor, "You gotta promise me one thing. No matter what happens in the next race, we go back to show business!"[110]

**Golf**

• Lots of old-time comedians took up golf after they became successful and started making money. The first 18 holes that Jimmy Durante ever played were a disaster, with Mr. Durante racking up a score of over 200. When Mr. Durante asked his partner what he should give the caddy, his partner replied, "Your clubs!"

Musicians also started playing golf after becoming successful. Hoagy Carmichael, composer of "Stardust" and "Georgia on My Mind," once got lucky on the Pebble Beach golf course and hit a hole-in-one. Mr. Carmichael said, "I think I've got the idea now."

Talent agents do the same thing as comedians and musicians. Arthur Lake once started playing golf with a man who wanted to be a perfectionist. The man needed to make a 40-foot putt on the first hole, and he knelt behind the ball, then he paced the distance to the cup, then he held up his putter perpendicularly for some reason, then he went to the other side of the cup and looked at the ground between the cup and his ball, and then he picked and threw a little grass to see how the wind was blowing. At this point, Mr. Lake told him, "Congratulations. I concede the match. I cannot take 18 holes of this."

While playing at El Caballero, California, comedian Buddy Hackett hit his ball into a wooded, marshy area. His caddy advised him, "Take a club." Mr. Hackett asked, "How do I know what club to take? I can't see what the lie is." The caddy replied, "Any club will do. It's for the snakes." And Mr. Hackett was playing golf with fellow comedian Sam Levinson when Mr. Levenson hit one, two, three balls into the water. Mr. Hackett asked, "Sam, why don't you use an old ball?" Mr. Levenson replied, "Buddy, I never get any."[111]

- While growing up in pre-World War II Britain, Ian Fleming (the author of the James Bond books) occasionally played golf with his mother and their friends. After playing a round of golf, his mother used to tip the caddy with the gift of a toothbrush.[112]

**Good Deeds**

- Comedian Jack Benny was noted for his professional generosity to other entertainers. Singer Abbe Lane worked with Mr. Benny in a theater-in-the-round, and before the opening they looked at letters on the marquee. Ms. Lane's contract stated that her name would appear at "100 percent billing" — this refers to the size of the letters on the marquee. However, "The Jack Benny Show" appeared in 100 percent, while "and starring Abbe Lane" appeared in 75 percent. Mr. Benny looked at the marquee and said, "No, no, no, that will never do." Immediately, Ms. Lane thought that Mr. Benny, who was a huge star (and obviously his name should appear first), was going to insist that her name appear in smaller letters, but he said, "I want this changed. I want it to read 'The Jack Benny and Abbe Lane Show.'" She did the first half of the show, and Mr. Benny did the second half of the show. In addition to singing, Ms. Lane spoke about shopping at Neiman-Marcus. Mr. Benny also had jokes about Neiman-Marcus, and Ms. Lane told him, "Jack, I just feel awful, because if I make any references to Neiman-Marcus, it's going to take the edge off what you do." Mr. Benny replied, "Don't be silly. I have lots of other things that I could say, so you do it." Ms. Lane remembered later, "And then he improved on what I had to say. I can't think of another performer in the world who would do that. It was the most wonderful engagement. I felt that I had finally arrived and was working with the best of the best."[113]

- Joseph Barbera and William Hanna are famous for their Hanna-Barbera cartoons, featuring such stars as Yogi Berra, Huckleberry Hound, and — of course — the Flintstones. They also made cartoons featuring Tom and Jerry that showed before movies. Mr.

Barbera once visited an ill boy at the request of nurses in the pediatric ward — Mr. Barbera called them "wonderful, caring, dedicated people." This boy was depressed and withdrawn, and his mother had not seen him in six months. Mr. Barbera talked to the boy about Tom and Jerry and drew pictures of Tom and Jerry for him. The boy ended up smiling and laughing; the nurses ended up crying. One nurse told Mr. Barbera that it was "the most incredible, moving experience" of her entire professional life.

In his old age, Mr. Barbera invited forty of his colleagues to dinner at his favorite Chinese restaurant — a way to say thanks to them. At one point, Mel Blanc, who provided the voices for so many Hanna-Barbera characters, stood up and said, "I've known Joe Barbera for thirty years, and I want to say that I have never heard in all that time one person say one bad thing about him." Mr. Barbera said, "I have never been prouder, happier, or more pleased with myself than at that moment."[114]

- When playwright Robert E. Sherwood was just starting out in life, he was given a job on Vanity Fair, where he worked alongside Robert Benchley and Dorothy Parker. Since then, his advice to young people hoping to be a success has been, "Merely make sure that you start out in fast company."

Mr. Sherwood's friends were wits. While Mr. Sherwood's friend Mr. Benchley worked for *Vanity Fair*, he was required to fill out a card giving an excuse every time he was late for work—a policy he regarded as childish. One day, Mr. Benchley arrived late, then wrote on the card that he had been delayed because he had helped to round up a herd of elephants had escaped from the Hippodrome.

Marc Connelly and Robert Benchley were walking down the street on either side of the very tall Robert E. Sherwood, when they saw a man on stilts advertising something on signs covering his front and back like a sandwich. Mr. Connelly and Mr. Benchley immediately squatted, then looked up at Mr. Sherwood and asked, "What are you advertising?"

Robert E. Sherwood was wounded during World War I—he was shot in the legs and suffered from gas poisoning. Robert Benchley was surprised that "Mr. Sherwood, who was six-feet-seven inches tall—was shot in the legs, so he developed the theory that Mr. Sherwood had been lying on the ground and waving his legs in the air. Mr. Sherwood denied this."[115]

- In 1885, when Walt Whitman, the poet who wrote *Leaves of Grass*, was old, many people contributed $10 each to buy him a horse and a buggy so that he could take rides in it. Some people admired Mr. Whitman not for his poetry, but for his good deeds such as taking care of soldiers during the Civil War. Boston author Oliver Wendell Holmes regarded Whitman's verses, which sometimes referred to sex, as "among the most cynical instances of indecent exposure I recollect." However, he also said that Mr. Whitman "served well the cause of humanity, and I do not begrudge him a ten dollar bill."

During the Civil War, Mr. Whitman assisted during amputations, and he cleaned and bandaged wounds. When a soldier requested rice pudding, he paid a woman to cook it. And on a hot day, he bought ice cream for the wounded soldiers in a ward.

When he was a young man, Mr. Whitman made friends of the people who drove stagecoaches on Broadway. Once, a driver became ill. Mr. Whitman did the driving for him, and then he gave the money he had earned to the driver's family.

Perhaps Mr. Whitman was influenced by a good deed performed by the Marquise de Lafayette on 4 July 1825, when Walt was a boy. Lafayette was in Brooklyn to lay a cornerstone for what would be a library. He entered the large hole that would be the cellar of the library, and he lifted down a number of children — Walt included — into the large hole so that they could watch the ceremony. Walt felt "childish pride" because he was "one of those who were taken in the arms of Lafayette."[116]

• Very early in his career, Jimmy Durante played piano in a bar called Diamond Tony's, which was named after the owner, who wore fake diamond rings. Once Diamond Tony was robbed by a man who took his wallet and pocket watch, but who told him, "You can keep those phony diamonds. My wife just bought better ones in a dollar store." The bar was frequented by prostitutes, whom Mr. Durante always treated with respect. He said, "Sure, I knew they was fallen ladies. But still they was females. An' to me that's sacred." One prostitute went to Hollywood and found some success in legitimate movies. Unfortunately, a fan magazine found out about her past and printed a story about it. She called Mr. Durante, who worried that she would think that it was he who had told the reporter about her past. She said on the telephone, "I didn't think that for a minute. I knew you wouldn't do a thing like that. The rat who squealed was an old boyfriend." Mr. Durante said later, "That poor girl was a good kid who just had a lot of bad breaks." Years later, she told a reporter, "Schnozzola was the only decent person in Diamond Tony's. He almost restored my faith in men, even if he kept refusing the freebies I offered him." Another prostitute was Gladie, who borrowed from him a ring that his mother had given him; it had belonged to her grandmother. Gladie disappeared for a while, and then she returned. Mr. Durante said, "She tells me she hocked the ring to pay for a certain kind of ladies' operation but promises to get it back." Then she disappeared again and did not come back. Years later, when she had stopped looking beautiful and had started looking cadaverous, she saw him again and kissed him. He did not know who she was until she introduced herself. She died — of malnutrition. Her worldly possessions fit in a paper bag: a crucifix, a map of Florida, some torn lingerie, and a bundle of clippings about Mr. Durante. On her paperwork, she listed him as next of kin. He paid for her funeral.

Mr. Durante spoke well of most people, including members of the Mafia. He, and other people on the Lower East Side who grew up at the time that Mr. Durante did, knew about many good deeds that members of the Mafia performed. He told a story about a woman whose daughter was hit by a trolley car and crippled. Next the woman's husband got the big C (cancer) and died. Then the woman's son, who painted houses to get money for the family to live on, fell off a ladder and was crippled. The landlord was ready to evict the family. Mr. Durante said, "That's when the Mafia marches in. Not only do they make the landlord change his mind, but give the lady each month some regular money to live on. I could tell you plenty of stories like that one. Sure, I know those men do lots of terrible things, but it's hard for me to hate someone from what I see with my own eyes."

Mr. Durante, as you would expect, did his share of good deeds. When the stock market fell in October 1929, he lost a lot of money, but fortunately he was making a lot of money as an entertainer. When he read about a mother who was forced to feed her hungry little daughter dog food, he visited the mother and gave her $50 — a lot of money back then.[117]

- Eric Blair completed a manuscript he titled *A Scullion's Diary*, about his travels as a tramp, but it was rejected frequently, including by such luminaries as T.S. Eliot, and he gave up on getting it published. Therefore, he gave it to a friend, Mabel Fierz, and told her to keep the paper clips but to get rid of the manuscript. Fortunately, Mabel was interested in literature and writers, and she gave it to a literary agent, Leonard Moore, who agreed to represent Mr. Blair. The manuscript was published as *Down and Out in Paris and London*, and Mr. Blair took the pseudonym George Orwell and wrote *Animal Farm* and *1984*. The manuscript of *Animal Farm* was nearly destroyed in a bombing attack on London by Germany in World War II. Fortunately, Mr. Blair retrieved the manuscript from the wreckage left by a bomb.[118]

- Franklin Ajaye met fellow comedian Flip Wilson a few times after Flip had retired with a big pile of money. The last time that Franklin saw him, Flip had driven his motorcycle to a Roscoe's Chicken and Waffles. Flip bought breakfast for everybody.

Another black comedian who did good deeds was Redd Foxx, star of TV's *Sanford and Son*. White comedian Tom Dreesen remembers, "Redd would look all over. If he saw anybody that didn't have any money and they couldn't pay their SAG or their AFTRA insurance, he would take them to the show and tell the writers, 'Write 'em in, put them on the show. Let 'em get one line.' He'd make sure it was a speaking line. That way, he had to pay different [more] money. Redd did that time and time and time again."

By the way, in the early days of sampling, samples were not paid for — it took a while for people to realize that samples need to be legally cleared. Reynaldo Rey once heard a sample from one of his albums on one of Ice Cube's albums, so he went to Ice Cube's trailer — Ice Cube was filming the movie *Friday* — and said, "Hey, man, you owe me some money. I'm on one of your albums." Reynaldo said that Ice Cube "laughed and invited me in, paid for it, and put me in the movie. Good dude."

In a conversation about Dave Chappelle, fellow comedian Bob Sumner said that Dave is a hero. In his book *Black Comedians on Black Comedy*, Darryl Littleton quoted him, "Great guy. I know stories about Dave that's a lot deeper than just being a comedian. He's a Good Samaritan. Him and David Edwards saved a little girl from being apprehended on a Washington subway one time. They were hanging out late after a gig one night and they noticed this guy had this girl on the subway and this girl was giving them like, y'know, little things that something wasn't right. They come to find out she was being kidnapped and Dave [Chappelle] and Dave [Edwards] actually got the girl to break loose, y'know, and then they got the guy."[119]

- Rosie O'Donnell has been incredibly generous. Ms. O'Donnell helped Jaren Millard, a Hollywood hairdresser and makeup artist in 1997, when he was recovering from pneumonia. Mr. Millard said, "Not only did Rosie pay my medical bills, but after I was released from the hospital — and had no place to go — she flew me in her own private jet to her Florida home and provided for my round-the-clock nursing care. Until the time I was back on my feet and able to care for myself, she continued to help me. If not for her, I would've been out on the streets or in a shelter. And I knew a hairdresser whom she moved into her home after he was stricken with AIDS. He stayed there — and she paid all his bills — until his death. I have also met several women battling breast cancer whom Rosie has helped." Mr. Millard added, "Lots of stars are happy to lend their name to or donate money to a cause. They're happy to have the press coverage, but most don't want to become personally involved. Rosie is not like that. She not only gives the money directly — she also stays in constant touch with you, wanting to know how you are doing. She really cares and doesn't ask for anything in return." She also helped Jason Opsahl, her co-star in *Grease* on Broadway, when he developed a brain tumor. She paid for his medical care, and for his food and rent when he could not work after he left the hospital. He died on 25 October 2002, at age 39. Mr. Opsahl's mother, Muriel, said, "Jason had many friends who loved him. But Rosie was a special friend. She even sat with us at the funeral service, like family."[120]
- Franz Kafka died at age 40 of tuberculosis, but even when he knew that he was dying, he performed a notable good deed. While he was walking in a park in Berlin, Germany, he saw a little girl who was crying because she had lost a doll. Franz told her that the doll was not lost, but was instead living an exciting new life after having met a boy doll. The little girl wanted proof of this, so Franz wrote a long letter that was supposedly from the doll, and the next day he went to the park and gave it to the little girl. He wrote letters from the doll every day for

three weeks and gave each letter to the little girl; by that time, the little girl was over the loss of the doll. (In the letters, the girl doll married the boy doll.)[121]

• David Lodge, a British actor, was in the British Air Force in 1945; he and others provided entertainment for the troops. He was 23, and another entertainer was only 19. Mr. Lodge noticed a big Welshman picking on the 19-year-old. Mr. Lodge had a big piece of iron that he was using to stir ashes in a wood- or coal-burning stove, and he told the big Welshman to leave the 19-year-old alone. Mr. Lodge was dissatisfied with the big Welshman's reply, so he gave the big piece of iron to the 19-year-old and said that if he needed to, he ought to hit the big Welshman with the big piece of iron — "And if you don't, I will." The big Welshman then stopped picking on the 19-year-old, who turned out to be comic Peter Sellers, who was later the star of *Being There* and the Pink Panther movies. Mr. Lodge and Mr. Sellers made several films together, and when Mr. Lodge's mother grew ill with cancer, Mr. Sellers arranged for her to see the best cancer doctors. Mr. Sellers paid for this, and Mr. Lodge believes that his mother got another 15 months of life because of it.[122]

• Very early in his career, Don Barnhart, Jr., bombed — and bombed badly. In fact, he bombed so badly that he told the audience, "Thanks for putting up with me. You probably won't ever see me again." This exit line got him his biggest laugh of the night. Don felt very bad, and comedian George Wallace came over and asked him, "How'd it go?" Don said, "Didn't you just *see* that? What do you think?" George said, "It doesn't matter what I think. It matters what *you* think, Donny boy. Tonight was the best thing that could have happened to you. You will now either get out of the business and lead a normal life, or you'll work so hard this will never happen again." Jump ahead 15 years. Don is a professional comic, and he is appearing at the Montreal Comedy Festival. A young comic has just bombed and is shaking and crying. Don asks him, "How'd it go?" The young comic says, "Didn't you just *see* that? I just took a nosedive in front of everybody." Don then says, "Did I ever tell you what George Wallace said to me?"[123]

• Carol Burnett is an incredibly nice person, as this story illustrates. In 1964, she took a taxi in New Year City. She paid her fare and left a tip, got out of the taxi, and closed the door. Unfortunately, the door had closed on her coat, the taxi driver did not know that, and the taxi driver started driving away. Fortunately, traffic made the taxi move slowly, and Carol was able to avoid being dragged by the taxi by running alongside it. A passerby saw what had happened and waved at the taxi driver to stop. The taxi driver was horrified, and he asked Carol if she was OK. Carol said, "Yes. How much extra do I owe you?"[124]

• When cartoon director Chuck Jones was a child, he lived near the Hollywood Bowl. He and other children would climb down the side of a hill and listen to and watch the entertainments for free. One guard was assigned to watch the side of the hill, and he knew that the children were there. Because the guard was a nice man, he would always do such things as whistle or walk into bushes to let the children know about his presence so that they could hide and not get caught.[125]

• Caitlin Moran, British author of *How to Be a Woman*, loves Twitter. She also finds it useful in solving emergencies. For example, in 2011 someone stole her brother's wallet while he was at Victoria station. Ms. Moran said, "I just went on Twitter and asked if there was anyone nearby who could go and give him a fiver so he could get the tube [subway] to my house. And within 12 minutes, someone had."[126]

**Hecklers**

• Bill Maher remembers that after he had appeared on *The Tonight Show with Johnny Carson* the very first time, he appeared at a gig in the South. He told a joke that bombed, then said, "Johnny Carson loved that joke last night." A deep Southern voice replied, "Well, Johnny ain't here tonight." In 1960, comedian Shelley Berman was heckled and he quickly put the heckler down with a comic insult. The heckler did not like being laughed at, and he stood up and said, "Come outside and say that." Milton Berle, a famous comedian in the audience, said, "Shelley's busy, but I'll go outside with you." Shelley remembers, "The audience went wild."[127]

• After a heckler punched Scottish comedian Gerry Sadowitz on stage, comedians Denis Leary and Bill Hicks were asked by the media for their opinion about the incident. Mr. Hicks said, "You should never attack anybody *ever* under any circumstances." Mr. Leary added, "The good thing is if somebody actually takes a shot at me or Hicks, it's just gonna be a gunshot from the audience. They won't even bother to come up on stage." Mr. Hicks agreed, "We get a different class of hecklers."[128]

**Humor**

• Artist James Montgomery Flagg painted Mark Twain's portrait although at first Mr. Twain said that he would "rather have smallpox than sit for his picture." Of course, Mr. Twain told funny stories during his sittings and at times Mr. Flagg could not paint because he was laughing so hard. Mr. Flagg remembers that once Mr. Twain cussed softly and then said, "My wife cusses, too — not the same words. *She* says 'Sugar!' and the Recording Angel will give her just as black marks as he does me!" One of Mr. Twain's eccentricities was to spread his mail in a long line on the floor. He would walk down the line and choose the letters that he wanted to read. In his old age, Mr. Twain always wore white suits. He told Mr. Flagg, "I don't like to be conspicuous, but I *do* like to be the most noticeable person!" Mr. Twain and his friend William Dean Howells once attended a performance by singer Adelina Patti. Mr. Howells asked him what he thought of Ms. Patti, and Mr. Twain replied, "I would rather sleep with that woman stark naked than with General Grant in full uniform."[129]

• Nathaniel Hawthorne, author of *The Scarlet Letter*, is not usually thought of as being funny, but he had his moments. When he finally felt that he could no longer write, he wrote his editor James Fields in February 1864 and announced his retirement. He also gave Mr. Fields this suggestion for announcing his retirement in the *Atlantic Monthly*: "Mr. Hawthorne's brain is addled at last, and much to our satisfaction, he tells us that he cannot possibly go on with the Romance [*The Dolliver Romance*] announced on the cover of the Jan. magazine." Mr. Hawthorne added in his note to Mr. Fields, "Say anything you like, in short, though I really don't think the Public will care what you say." As a young boy, he complained in a letter about his grandmother forcing him to eat rotting oranges: "We have to eat the bad ones first, as the good are to be kept until they are spoilt also." Mr. Hawthorne died on 12 May 1864.[130]

**Husbands and Wives**

• The father of Dick King-Smith, the author of *Babe: The Gallant Pig*, had a habit of saying the wrong thing. After Dick's wife had given birth to their second child (both children were daughters), Dick's father said to her, "Wrong sex again, eh, Myrle?" Dick writes that his father "earned himself an earful from his furious daughter-in-law." Before Dick and his wife were married, she was very resourceful. She once tried to visit Dick, who had been wounded during World War II, but she discovered that he had suddenly been moved to another hospital. She had a long trip home, no return ticket, and not enough money to buy a return ticket. So she played poker with some officers and won enough money to pay for her return trip. By the way, even earlier when she met him for the first time as an adult (they had known each other as children before one of their families moved), she was worried that she would blush when she saw him, so she used a powder that her friends said would hide blushes. But when Dick looked at her, he noticed that her face was green.[131]

• Howard Jacobson allows his wife, television producer Jenny de Yong, to read his manuscripts before anyone else does. While she is reading them in her study, he will sometimes listen to find out if she is crying or laughing. He said, "There's only one novel [*The Act of Love*] where she's said, 'This could be the end of our marriage, but this book isn't working.' I called the publisher and said they'd have to wait a bit longer for it."[132]

• Danny Thomas' heritage was Lebanese, and when he wanted to get married to a woman named Rosie, he had not quite won over her father. In fact, Rosie's father told her, "If you marry that Turk, you're gonna end up in a tent." For his 25th wedding anniversary, Danny rented a huge tent and held a huge party at his house in Beverly Hills. Many people, including celebrities, were there, and Jack Haley was the master of ceremonies. When Jack called on Danny to make a toast, Danny turned to his father-in-law and said, "Pa, do you remember when you said to Rosie twenty-five years ago, 'If you marry that Turk, you'll end up in a tent?' Well, here we are."[133]

• Humorist H. Allen Smith was once driving while his wife was reading the roadmap and navigating. She told him that she had discovered a "superhighway" on the map that would take them in a straight line directly to Chicago. Mr. Smith stopped the car, looked at the map, and discovered that the "superhighway" was the state line dividing Illinois from Indiana.[134]

• Stephenie Meyer, author of *Twilight*, is a Mormon, and her husband is a Mormon. Unfortunately, many people don't know a lot about Mormonism. For example, someone once asked her, "So, how many wives can your husband have?" Ms. Meyer replied, "Just one, if he wants to keep the one he already has."[135]

• Mark Twain once attended a dinner at the White House, but his wife, Olivia, stayed home; however, she told him not to wear his winter galoshes at the dinner. Mr. Twain attended the dinner and did not wear his galoshes. He also got the President's wife, Frances Cleveland, to sign a card that said, "He didn't."[136]

**Illnesses and Injuries**

• After political cartoonist Herblock received an honorary Doctor of Laws degree from Lake Forest, he remarked that since he now had all the "rights and privileges appertaining thereto" the degree, he might start filing lawsuits. The president of Lake Forest then told him a story about humorist Stephen Leacock, who had also received an honorary doctorate. He signed his name as Dr. Stephen Leacock when he boarded a ship for Europe. During the voyage, a ship officer came to his cabin and told him that a beautiful Ziegfeld Follies showgirl had sprained her hip and could he please examine her. Mr. Leacock said, "I was down there like a shot, but not soon enough — two doctors of divinity had got there before me."[137]

• Harry Crane was a radio comedy writer who suffered from diabetes. Once, he was at Nate 'n' Al's delicatessen when he felt an attack coming on and knew that he immediately needed some fruit to get sugar in his system, so he went to the counter and asked for an orange. However, the counterman refused to give him an orange because it wasn't Mr. Crane's turn to be served — with the result that Mr. Crane collapsed, became unconscious, and had to be taken to a hospital. One of his friends heard what had happened, and called him at the hospital, saying he wanted to visit and asking how to get there. "It's easy," said Mr. Crane. "You go to Nate 'n' Al's and ask for an orange."[138]

• On 12 December 1983, science and science-fiction writer Isaac Asimov had a heart bypass operation. His greatest fear was he would suffer brain damage if his brain did not get enough oxygen during the operation, so he asked his physician to make sure that his brain was well supplied with oxygen. After the operation, his physician tested Mr. Asimov's brain for damage by saying, "Make me up a limerick, Isaac. Mr. Asimov replied, "There once was an old doctor named Paul / With a penis exceedingly small …." His physician interrupted, "That's enough, Isaac. You pass." Mr. Asimov once received a compliment from a librarian who said that Mr. Asimov's books were the ones most often stolen from the library.[139]

- Don Imus hosted a radio show on which his friend the country musician and author Kinky Friedman occasionally appeared. In June 2000 Mr. Imus was thrown by a horse and suffered severe injuries: 17 broken ribs, a punctured lung, and a broken clavicle. He was in an isolated area, and paramedics could not reach him for two hours. After recovering — slowly — Mr. Imus said on his radio show that the two hours he had spent waiting for the paramedics were the longest two hours of his life. A listener called in and said that the longest two hours of *his* life were whenever Mr. Imus' show featured Kinky Friedman.[140]
- Reporter Clark Mollenhoff once had a successful brain operation. Afterward, while in a hospital bed he wrote a letter to a friend at the *New Orleans Times-Picayune* — a friend whose real name happened to be Edgar Allen Poe. Mr. Mollenhoff's doctor stopped by his room and asked him what he was doing. When Mr. Mollenhoff replied, "I'm writing a letter to Edgar Allen Poe," the doctor's face clearly indicated that he was thinking, "Where did I go wrong?"[141]
- Whenever comedian Jackie Gleason got overly obese, he would check himself into a hospital for a strict, medically supervised diet. Writer Leonard Stern once went to visit him in the hospital, but the nurse told him, "I'm sorry. Mr. Gleason wasn't feeling well, and he went home."[142]

**Insults**

- Conductor Otto Klemperer was a good man with an insult. He once conducted Richard Strauss' *Der Rosenkavalier*, with Lotte Lehmann, about whom English classical music producer Walter Legge once wrote, "That glorious artist who instinctively poured out warm radiance and impulsive femininity was not the most accurate of singers." Mr. Klemperer corrected her a few times, and Ms. Lehmann complained, "Don't keep on interrupting me! I'm only singing a few performances here, and then I'm off to sing it at Covent Garden, then at the Chicago Opera." Mr. Klemperer then said, "Strauss or the Lehmann version?"

He once kept an orchestra rehearsing after the rehearsal was supposed to end, and the first violinist kept looking at his watch. Mr. Klemperer asked the violinist, "Is it still going?" Then he continued the rehearsal.

When Mr. Klemperer heard that a rival distinguished conductor had died, he sometimes said, "We are having quite a good year."

Mr. Klemperer was loyal. Mr. Legge once asked him whether he considered Gustav Mahler to be a better artist than Anton Bruckner. Mr. Klemperer replied, "Of course not." Mr. Legge then asked, "Then why do you play more Mahler than Bruckner?" Mr. Klemperer, who was born a Jew, replied, "Because Mahler was a Jew and because he got me my first jobs."

Mr. Klemperer, who had converted to Catholicism, once complained to Zvi Haftel, the leader of the Israel Philharmonic Orchestra, about never being invited to conduct the orchestra. Mr. Haftel replied, "Dr. Klemperer, you have chosen to be received into the Roman Catholic Church — so for us you are a heretic." Mr. Klemperer said, "But my colleague, Dr. Koussevitsky, is also a Jew who was baptized, and he has not only conducted your orchestra here, [but] he has also toured with it in the United States." Mr. Haftel said, "Yes, but Dr. Koussevitsky conducted without fee." Mr. Klemperer replied, "I am still Jewish enough not to do that."[143]

• One of the best things about being witty is being able to come up with exactly the right insult. Dick Cavett and his friend David Lloyd once worked with a comedy writer who suffered from a lack of a decent personality as well as a lack of writing talent. Mr. Cavett once heard his friend tell the loathed writer, "Your parents owe the world a retraction." And when the two saw the loathed writer come out of the men's room, Mr. Cavett remarked, "That's where he puts his best stuff on paper." As many creative people do, Mr. Cavett occasionally suffers from depression. A man once told him, "Depression is for sniveling little neurotics." Mr. Cavett replied, "How, then, have you escaped it?"[144]

• Gertrude Atherton was born in San Francisco, California, and she was a very popular novelist in England. She left Bodley Head for another publishing company: Sands & Company. John Lane, the Bodley Head publisher, wanted her to come back to his company, so he told her, "I will go down on my knees to you if you will come back." She replied, "Get down, Lane — get down on your knees." He did, but she did not come back to Bodley Head. Instead, she told Mr. Lane, "Very pretty, Lane. Very touching. Now get up — and go drop yourself in the Thames."[145]

• Groucho Marx once attended a baseball game in which a poor-hitting California Angels second baseman managed to reach second base after he and a fellow player were walked. Groucho commented, "That's the first time I've seen that guy on second without his glove." Groucho once attended a party that honored a famous actress. He gave her this toast: "I toast your beauty, your talent, your charm, your wit — which gives you a rough idea of how hard up a man can be for a drink."[146]

**Language**

• Comic playwright and actor Roy Smiles grew up in England while the TV show *Porridge* was appearing in 1974-1977. *Porridge* was set in a prison, so you would expect it to have swear words. However, because of the time it appeared on TV, it could not use real swear words, so the writers invented their own swear words. For example, an actor would say "naff off" instead of "f*ck off" and "nerk" instead of "Berkshire Hunt" ("Berkshire Hunt" is an example of rhyming slang — the phrase rhymes with the word that is meant). Young Ron and his classmates learned the fake swear words from the TV show, and they used them at school. Because the swear words were fake swear words, no one at the school stopped them from using them. The adult Roy Smiles remembers this and says, "Absolutely bloody marvelous!"

Mr. Smiles admires the old-time English comic Tommy Trinder, who was a master at putting down hecklers. For example, on stage, Mr. Trinder said, "Trinder's the name; there'll never be another." Orson Welles, who disliked Mr. Trinder, shouted, "Why don't you change it then?" Mr. Trinder replied, "Is that a proposal of marriage?"

Another comedian, Max Miller, believed that Mr. Trinder was stealing his style and his jokes. Seeing Mr. Trinder in the audience of one of his shows, Mr. Miller asked him, "Are you getting all this down?" Mr. Trinder replied, "Could you speak a little slower?"

Mr. Smiles admired this quip by Beatle John Lennon: When an interviewer asked Mr. Lennon whether Ringo Starr was the best drummer in the world, Mr. Lennon replied, "He's not even the best drummer in the Beatles."[147]

- Paul Krugman, Nobel Prize winner in Economics in 2008 and professor at Princeton, is a good writer both in his *New York Times* column and in his *New York Times* blog. I have read some of his books for the general public and enjoyed them, but I am not educated enough in economics to understand his industrial-strength economics papers. He moderates his *New York Times* blog and so occasionally reminds commenters of some rules of civility in commenting, such as this one: "Obscenity will get your comment deleted; I suspect that a fair number of commenters don't even realize they're doing it, because that's the way many of us #$%^! talk these days. But think about it, and don't waste your time or mine."

Mr. Krugman also wants a certain amount of accuracy in choice of words. For example, he writes, "Get your insults right. There is, I believe, a fair bit of evidence against the hypothesis that I'm stupid. What you mean to say is that I'm evil."[148]

- Goodman Ace wrote comedy, and he understood how important it is to use the right words in the right order when creating comedy.

Columnist Walter Winchell once asked Mr. Ace about very popular (and number one in the ratings) comedian Jack Benny, "You know Jack Benny very well, don't you? Tell me, why does he always look so worried?" Mr. Ace replied, "I don't know, Mr. Winchell — maybe it's because he's afraid he'll drop all the way down to second place." Mr. Winchell wrote down the quote, but he left out "all the way," so Mr. Ace begged him to add those words. Mr. Winchell did not, and so he ruined a perfectly good joke. Mr. Ace said later, "Jack would have known that each word was important — and would have placed them properly in the sentence."[149]

• In 1939, an alumnus of MIT, class of 1889, wrote a 50,110-word novelty novel titled *Gadsby*. Why "novelty"? It did not contain the letter E. It did include sentences such as this: "Youth cannot stay for long in a condition of inactivity."[150]

# Chapter 4: From Letters to Poetry

**Letters**
- Maurice Sendak, who died on 8 May 2012, wrote and illustrated many books for children. Of course, he received letters from his readers. He liked the ones that were actually voluntarily written by the kids — adults assigned too many of the letters he received. He gave an example: "Dear Mr. Sendak, Mrs. Markowitz said would you please send a free book and two drawings?" But the ones from children who actually felt the urge to write him were wonderful and wonderfully honest — Mr. Sendak appreciated honesty. After he wrote *Outside Over There*, a little girl from Canada read it and wrote him, "I like all of your books, why did you write this book, this is the first book I hate. I hate the babies in this book, why are they naked, I hope you die soon. Cordially..." Her mother wrote this note that accompanied the letter: "I wondered if I should even mail this to you — I didn't want to hurt your feelings." Mr. Sendak's feelings were not hurt. He said, "I was so elated. It was so natural and spontaneous. The mother said, 'You should know I am pregnant and she has been fiercely opposed to it.' Well, she [the little girl] didn't want competition, and the whole book was about a girl who's fighting against having to look after her baby sister." Mr. Sendak added, "If [the letter is] true, then you can't care about the vicious and the painful. You can only be astonished. Most kids don't dare tell the truth. Kids are the politest people in the world. A letter [that says, 'I hope you die soon'] is wonderful. 'I wish you would die.' I should have written back, 'Honey, I will.'"[151]
- In the year 2009 was the 50th anniversary of the publication of Evan S. Connell's novel *Mrs. Bridge*. Back when Mr. Connell began writing in the 1950s, he realized that he would receive many, many rejection letters. Like many other young authors, he taped them to a wall. He says, "I got up to something like 115 and thought, 'This is going to go on forever,' and so I stopped." Although he realizes that

in the future people will probably read books on screens, he still uses old-fashioned technology. He says, "I'm strictly low-tech myself. I use two Olympia typewriters that were made sometime in the '50s. They last forever, those things. They don't break down, and I don't have to fool around with digital stuff."[152]

• In 1936, novelist William Saroyan wrote H.L. Mencken, editor of *The American Mercury*, a polite letter asking for advice about starting a magazine. Mr. Mencken wrote back with this reply: "Dear Saroyan, I note what you say about your aspiration to edit a magazine. I am sending you by this mail a six-chambered revolver. Load it and fire every one into your head. You will thank me after you get to hell and learn from other editors there how dreadful their job was on earth."[153]

• John Train, a co-founder of *The Paris Review*, once lent his name as a reference for a young woman. One day, he received a letter from the American Library, asking him to contact the young woman and ask her to return five overdue books. Mr. Train handwrote a letter back that said, "I am sorry to be writing you in my own hand, but the machine on which I am used to compose these letters was last seen in the hands of [the young woman]."[154]

• Sometimes Mark Twain was slow in answering letters. Once a friend wanted a quick reply from Mr. Twain, so he enclosed in his letter some paper and a stamp. Very quickly, a postcard arrived from Mr. Twain: "Thanks for the sheet of writing paper and the stamp. Please send an envelope."[155]

**Media**

• One of the colorful characters whom political cartoonist Herblock knew was Harry Grayson, who loved New York and hated Cleveland, Ohio. After Mr. Grayson had been transferred to and moved to Cleveland, a tourist asked him for directions: "What is the quickest way out of town?" Mr. Grayson replied, "If I knew, I'd take it myself."

Someone once gave him a ride home. That someone followed Mr. Grayson's directions but soon realized that he was driving around in circles. He asked Mr. Grayson, "Harry, exactly which is your house?" Mr. Grayson, who was looking out the window, replied, "I don't know. I never saw it in the daytime before." He once tried to look up the spelling of a word and complained, "D*mn dictionary, you can't find anything in it." Herblock looked at the "dictionary" — it was a telephone book.

At a Florida hotel, Mr. Grayson complained about the noise. A hotel manager listened to the "noise" and said, "That's the surf, Mr. Grayson." At a different hotel, Mr. Grayson ordered a well-done steak from room service. He did not like the steak, so he threw it out a window. When hotel management asked if he were the one who had thrown a steak out a window, Mr. Grayson replied, "Yes, and do you call that steak well done?"[156]

• Back in the days of Prohibition, a cub reporter on the *New York Tribune* was assigned to write an article about the arrival of the Barnum & Bailey Circus. He got the assignment because the circus would arrive at 4 a.m., and none of the veteran reporters wanted to be up that early. Like many city reporters during Prohibition, this cub reporter drank alcohol at a speakeasy. Although he had to be present at the arrival of the circus at 4 a.m., the reporter did not want to miss out on any drinking time, so he went to the speakeasy as usual and simply did not go home to sleep. At 4 a.m., he left the speakeasy, hailed a taxi, and told the driver, "Drive up Fifth Avenue until you see an elephant." During Prohibition, when many people ceased to drink moderately and instead drank immoderately as a form of protest, cab drivers sometimes got requests like this. This cab driver figured the passenger simply wanted to go up Fifth Avenue, so he started driving — and he was shocked to see an elephant and the rest of the Barnum & Bailey Circus parading down Fifth Avenue.[157]

- Jeff Kinney is the author of the Wimpy Kid humorous series of books, which appeal immensely to children. In fact, *Time* magazine named him one of the 100 most influential people of 2009, an assessment that Mr. Kinney disagreed with, saying, "I'm not even the most influential person in my own house." When he wrote the first Wimpy Kid book, he thought he was writing for adults: "I never thought I was writing for kids at all. It really shocked and unsettled me to hear kids were buying the books. If I'd known I was writing for kids, I might actually have spelt things out a bit more and that would probably have killed the appeal."[158]
- Mary Chase won a Pulitzer Prize for her comic play *Harvey*. Before marrying Bob Chase and becoming a playwright, Mary Coyle was a newspaper reporter for the *Denver Post*. Once, she arrived at a Denver home in which three of six family members had been killed in a drunken brawl, then introduced herself as a reporter to a bloodstained survivor. The man told her, "Go away. We've decided not to put anything about this in the papers."[159]
- In 1991, an editor on the city desk of the *Cleveland Plain Dealer* (Ohio) stated that reporters are a dime a dozen. The reporters responded by taping a dime on top of each of their computers. In 1993, Connie Schultz, then a future Pulitzer Prize-winner, started working for the *Plain Dealer*. She asked reporter Lou Mio about the dimes. He told her the story, and she asked, "Don't these dimes bother him?" Mr. Mio smiled and replied, "Every day."[160]
- Early in his career, H. Allen Smith was a member of the Denver Press Club. In 1949, after his membership had been lapsed for 19 years, he returned to Denver and spent a pleasant afternoon at the Press Club. A friend of his, Lee Casey, even gave him a new membership card — it was dated 19 years ahead. "We love you and want to see you again," Mr. Casey explained, "but only about once in 19 years."[161]
- For a few months in 1935, Evelyn Waugh was a correspondent for the *Daily Mail*, covering the Italian assault on Abyssinia. Only once

did he have a good story, and he wrote it in Latin (to keep the story a secret) and telegraphed it to the *Daily Mail*. Unfortunately, the people at the *Daily Mail* could not read Latin and assumed that the story was gibberish, and so they threw it away.[162]

**Mishaps**

• George Brown was a man who respected learning. When he was the Paramount Pictures publicity director, he hired a Harvard man named Bernie Kamins to work in the publicity department. Mr. Kamins' first assignment was to write the publicity releases for a cowboy movie. Since Mr. Kamins was an Easterner who knew nothing about cowboys, he looked at the publicity releases for a different Paramount cowboy movie to see if he could learn a few pointers. The first publicity release he read made reference to a "cowpike," which was a typo for a "cowpoke." Of course, Mr. Kamins didn't know that it was a typo, so in his publicity release, he also made reference to a cowpike. Later, someone complained to Mr. Brown about Mr. Kamins' use of "cowpike," but Mr. Brown said, "He's a Harvard man. If he says 'cowpike,' then 'cowpike' must be right."[163]

• Joseph Barbera of Hanna-Barbera fame once walked into a room in which were a friend named Sy Fisher and, unknown to him when he walked in and started talking, a VIP named Duke Ducovny. When he walked in the room, he smelled pipe tobacco and he saw Sy with a pipe. He said to Sy, "This is terrible. What kind of person would smoke a pipe? Pipes are an abomination. I can't stand pipes. ..." Then he saw Duke, who was also holding a lit pipe. He immediately pointed to Duke's pipe and continued, "...except that one. That, Duke, is one hell of a pipe, a great pipe, and that tobacco is straight from heaven. Sy, what's the matter with you? If you are going to smoke a pipe, why don't you take a lesson in class from Duke here? Get yourself a pipe just like his, ask him what kind of tobacco he's smoking, and buy yourself a load of it."[164]

- Jack Benny entertained the troops in Stuttgart, Germany, as part of a USO tour, but he did not know the protocol of being on a military base. Driving on the base, he saw some MPs waving at him, so he waved back, but he stopped driving when an MP shot at him and hit his jeep. The MPs checked his papers, discovered that Mr. Benny was supposed to be on the base, and then they examined his jeep. The MP who had shot at him said, "Loosened a spring." Fortunately, Mr. Benny was not injured. After the show, lots of soldiers surrounded Mr. Benny, requesting that he sign autographs. One soldier requested an autograph, then added, "Make mine a good one. I'm the soldier who shot at you."[165]

**Money**

- Gregory Maguire, author of *Wicked: The Life and Times of the Wicked Witch of the West*, has been very successful as a writer, but even he has been broke or nearly broke at times. Once, a man telephoned him to see if he could write a story for him. The man said, "I have an artist who does great drawings of animals in restaurants. I wonder if you could think of a story to go with the art." Mr. Maguire replied, "Of course not. That's not how a true artist works." Then he added, "By the way, how much would you pay?" Hearing the answer — $4,000 — Mr. Maguire said that he would think about it. And think he did. He says, "In ninety minutes I wrote a rhyming story about animals in restaurants." The man bought the story, and Mr. Maguire thought that he had figured out a great way to make money so he could do his own writing — simply write a few pieces like that each year and make some easy money. Unfortunately, he says, "Of course, I could never do it again. Ideas don't just come like that." Mr. Maguire once told his agent that he had some good ideas for stories, but he just couldn't come up with the few couple of words to start the stories. His agent replied, "I know what the first couple of words are: I'm broke."[166]

- Anita Loos, author of *Gentlemen Prefer Blondes*, was friends with Aldous Huxley, author of *Brave New World*. Mr. Huxley was, of course, a genius, but occasionally Ms. Loos felt superior to him. During the Battle of Britain in World War II, his income declined and so Ms. Loos got him an interview for a job as a Hollywood screenwriter. Mr. Huxley was offered a position, but he phoned Ms. Loos and said that he could not accept it. Why not? He explained, "Because it pays twenty-five hundred dollars a week. I simply cannot accept all that money to work in pleasant surroundings while all my family and friends are going hungry and being bombed in England." Ms. Loos asked, "Why can't you accept the money and send it to England?" After a short silence, Mr. Huxley's wife, Maria, got on the phone and said, "Anita, what would we ever do without you?" Ms. Loos replied, "The trouble with a genius like Aldous is that he just isn't very smart." Mr. Huxley once gave Ms. Loos a gift: perfume in a box shaped like a book. This is his note to her: "For Anita, one of the few books that doesn't stink." [167]

- Ed McMahon worked for many years with Jerry Lewis in the Muscular Dystrophy Telethon. His daughter Claudia worked for a year with the Muscular Dystrophy Association, and she was able to let him know that yes, the money the telethon raised was put to good use. She told her father, "I've never seen anything like it. I've never had to say no to a patient's request. Whatever they need — an electric wheelchair, a ramp built onto their home — the organization provides it for them without any red tape. It's the most incredible thing." Frank Sinatra once telephoned the telethon to donate $25,000, but the person answering the phone wondered whether Frank was really Frank. Because Ed McMahon knew Frank, he went to the phone to confirm Frank's identity. In their private life, the two men shared a toast. Frank would raise his glass and said, "To the festival." Ed would then say, "To the incredible festival of life." Therefore, Ed said on the phone, "To the what?" Frank replied, "To the festival," and Ed said to the telethoners, "Take his money."

Mr. McMahon idolized the great comedian W.C. Fields, about whom he knew many, many stories. One story was about a writer who requested permission to write Mr. Fields' biography. Mr. Fields told him, "Please do. Capital idea. Do it right away. I can't wait to see how it turns out."[168]

• Early in his career, George Carlin was funny and made a lot of money from conventional comedy. However, he was unhappy because he wanted to be funny and do comedy that also made a serious point. Finally, he got new management, one member of whom was Jeff Wald. It took a lot of hard work to get Mr. Carlin booked into the hip smaller clubs where he wanted to work because the management and audiences of those hip smaller clubs regarded Mr. Carlin as the kind of comedian who did Las Vegas and *The Ed Sullivan Show*. Eventually, Mr. Wald booked Mr. Carlin into a hip smaller club: It was a one-night stand-up show that got Mr. Carlin $250. Mr. Wald says, "I always say I took George Carlin from two hundred and fifty thousand dollars a year down to about twelve thousand dollars and improved his career." And Mr. Carlin did improve his career, becoming a comedian whom it is impossible to leave out of histories of comedy in the late twentieth century.[169]

• Zora Neale Hurston, author of *Their Eyes were Watching God*, was her own original person. She once took a nickel from the cup of a blind beggar, promising to pay it back but saying that she really needed the fare for the subway. A man once propositioned her on the elevator. She hit him hard, he fell on the floor, and when the elevator door opened, she walked away without looking back. As a creative person, she often lacked money. One day she was thrown out of her one-room house for non-payment of rent. She had a little money, but she decided to use it to buy new shoes because her old shoes resembled scraps. While she was in the shoe store, she received a telegram offering her a $200 advance for a book. She ran out of the shoe store wearing one old shoe and one new shoe in her hurry to get to a Western Union office and send a telegram accepting the offer.[170]

- Reynaldo Rey was a witness to how Redd Foxx treated comedians who borrowed money from him and did not want to pay it back. He once saw a comedian borrow $500 from Redd and promised to pay it back the following week, but the following week the comedian avoided Redd. The week after that, Redd tracked down the comedian and said, "Man, pay me my money." The comedian told him, "Man, don't be approaching me in public talking about that little p*ssy piece of money." And the comedian walked off without paying Redd. The week after that, Redd tracked down the comedian again. This time, Redd had a derringer. He took one bullet out of the derringer and slapped the comedian on the forehead with the bullet. The comedian asked, "What the h*ll was that about?" Redd said, "If you don't pay me my money, the next one will be coming much faster."[171]
- What Isaac Asimov most enjoyed in life was writing. Once Barbara Walters interviewed him, and she asked him off-camera what he liked to do other than write. But for Mr. Asimov, what he enjoyed most was writing and he did not greatly enjoy anything else. Finally, Ms. Walters asked him, "What if the doctors told you that you had only six months to live? What would you do then?" Mr. Asimov replied, "Type faster." Of course, Mr. Asimov made a great deal of money from his writing, although most writers don't. He was in a taxi once with a driver who asked what he did for a living. Ms. Asimov replied that he was a writer. The taxi driver told him, "I once wanted to be a writer, but I never got around to it." Mr. Asimov replied, "Just as well. You can't make a living as a writer." The taxi driver replied, "Isaac Asimov does."[172]
- Early in his career, comedian Jeff Foxworthy rode a New York subway while carrying $100 he had been paid for a show. He was worried about being mugged, so he messed up his hair, pulled out his shirt, and pretended to be drunk and mentally ill as he loudly babbled. The only bad thing that happened was that when he returned to his hotel room, his wife, Pamela Gregg, was scared by the way he looked.

Mr. Foxworthy once received an advance to do a TV show, but he decided not to do it because he disagreed with the producers about the format of the show. Although he was not legally obligated to do so, he refunded the advance. He then went on to do *The Jeff Foxworthy Show*, and when that show was cancelled, he helped many of the show's employees get new jobs.[173]

• Rich and famous comedian Danny Thomas, whose birth name was Amos Jacobs Kairouz and who was raised in Toledo, Ohio, once paid for tickets at a box-office booth, and when he received his change, he dropped a dime. Lots of people saw him drop the dime, and Danny was too embarrassed to pick it up. He thought, *I am Danny Thomas. I'm one of the world's top comedians. I've made millions. I'm not bending down to pick up that dime.* Then he reconsidered: *In reality, I'm Amos Jacobs of Toledo, Ohio, and Amos Jacobs knows how hard it is to make a dime.* He picked up the dime.[174]

• Comedian Dave Madden worked a couple of years on the *Laugh-In* show, which did an enormous amount of merchandising — including two comedy albums. When *Laugh-In* was finally cancelled, Mr. Madden received a check giving him his share of the merchandising profits. The check was for zero dollars and two cents. He laminated it and took it along as a comedy prop during visits to talk shows. (Mr. Madden says he didn't want to cash the check because his agent would have demanded his share of the profits.)[175]

• Early in his career, Jimmy Durante played piano at the Chatham Club in New York's Chinatown. Part of his job was to be on the lookout for customers trying to sneak away without paying their check. Each waiter was assigned a certain tune, and if Mr. Durante noticed a customer sneaking away, he would play the tune of the waiter assigned to that customer. When the waiter heard his tune, he knew one of his customers was trying to sneak out without paying.[176]

• Robert Harris' first novel, *Fatherland*, in which Germany has won World War II, was very successful, and he used the profits to pay off the mortgage on his house. He jokes, "It's been known ever since as The House That Hitler Bought." As an author, Mr. Harris is aware that comedians can often write well. His favorite joke is by Bob Monkhouse: "They laughed when I said I wanted to be a comedian. Well, they're not laughing now." Mr. Harris calls this joke "a masterpiece of brevity."[177]

- When Mike Nichols and Elaine May first came to New York in late 1957, they opened at the Village Vanguard. Basically, they were auditioning live in a room that was packed with people. Larraine Gordon was present, and she was laughing loud. Her husband, Max, the founder of the Village Vanguard, came over to her and requested, "Please don't laugh so loud. The[ir] agent is in the room, and the price is going to go up."[178]

- Two of Carl Sandburg's most famous poems are "Fog" and "Chicago." He worked as a reporter, and while he was in Grant Park on his way to interview a judge, he saw fog rolling into the harbor. The judge kept him waiting, and as he waited, he wrote "Fog." His poem "Chicago" won a $200 prize as the Best American Poem of the Year. Mr. Sandburg said that the cash prize would "just octuple our bank account."[179]

- Johnny Carson was married and divorced a number of times, and he paid out a lot of money in alimony. On *The Tonight Show*, Johnny performed some magic for a five-year-old — he made a quarter disappear and then he pulled it out of the boy's ear. The boy was impressed and asked, "How do you really make it disappear?" Johnny replied, "You get married."[180]

**Movies**

- Walt Disney was a story man: He knew what made a good story. When he decided to make a movie out of *Mary Poppins*, he read the book carefully. He gave a copy of the book to songwriters Richard and Robert Sherman and said, "My daughters and wife think this is very good. I read it and think there's a lot in it. Read this and tell me what you think." They quickly read it twice and then scheduled a meeting with Walt. The book was a series of short stories about Mary Poppins rather than a novel, so they chose the short stories that they thought would make a good movie. Walt listened to them for a while, and then he asked to look at their copy of the book. They had underlined the six chapters that they thought would work best as a movie. Walt then showed them his copy of the book. He had underlined the same six chapters that they had underlined.

Walt certainly knew his audiences. When his nephew's wife had a baby, Walt went to the hospital to see it. It was the middle of the Baby Boom and so lots of babies were there. Walt said, "Look at that! Seven years from now, they'll all be out there watching *Snow White*!" [181]

• In the 1994 movie *The Browning Version*, starring Albert Finney, the Greek schoolmaster he plays appears in a scene with schoolboys who are having trouble translating the ancient Greek of *Agamemnon* by the tragedian Aeschylus. Classicist Mary Beard points out that it is no wonder that they are having trouble: On each schoolboy's desk appears not an edition of Aeschylus in Greek, but instead a Penguin translation of Aeschylus into English. (Penguin books have instantly recognizable covers.) Ms. Beard writes, "Presumably some bloke in the props department had been sent off to find twenty copies of the *Agamemnon* and knew no better than to bring it in English."[182]

• Actor Sheldon Leonard — you know him as Nick the bartender in *It's a Wonderful Life*, once was asked to do a stunt that the director said was harmless. Mr. Leonard insisted that his stunt double be paid to be present and to advise him. The stunt double, who was a true professional when it came to dangerous stunts, came in, examined the stunt, and then turned to Mr. Leonard and said, "Don't do it."[183]

• When the original movie version of *The Producers* starring Zero Mostel and Gene Wilder was showing in theaters, a woman recognized creator Mel Brooks in an elevator. She told him, "Sir, I have seen your film and it is vulgar!" Mr. Brooks replied, "Madame, my film rises below vulgarity." (Film critic Roger Ebert, who was present, calls this his favorite Mel Brooks story.)[184]

**Music**

• Walter Legge, an English classical music producer, worked closely with soprano Maria Callas for 12 years. He and his wife, Elisabeth Schwarzkopf, greatly respected her. Mr. Legge first heard Ms. Callas sing in 1951 in Rome. He heard her sing the first act of *Norma* at the Rome Opera, and during an intermission he telephoned his wife to tell her that she needed to come to the Rome Opera right away and hear something exceptional. She, however, would not go: She had been listening to a radio broadcast of Ms. Callas singing arias, and she wanted to listen to the second half of the radio broadcast. When Ms. Schwarzkopf heard Ms. Callas sing Violetta in *La Traviata*, she told her, "There is no point in my singing this role again." And, in fact, she did not sing it again. Ms. Callas was very organized. Mr. Legge writes that all of her garments (and her handbags and gloves) in Milan, Italy, were tagged with notes on when she had bought them, how much they had cost, where and when she had worn them, and who had seen her wear them. She was critical of her singing. While recording for Mr. Legge, she asked him, "Walter, is that all right?" He replied, "Maria, it's marvelous." But Ms. Callas said, "I don't want to know if it's marvelous. Is it good?" (Mr. Legge wrote, "Callas had an absolute contempt for merely beautiful singing." Instead, she sought to convey dramatic meaning in her singing.) She could also be witty. She once met conductor Otto Klemperer, who both praised and criticized her: "I have heard you twice. *Norma*, very good. *Iphigénie* — horrible." Ms. Callas smiled and said, "Thank you, Maestro." Mr. Klemperer continued, "But I am sure Herr Legge will agree to invite you to sing at a concert here with me. What would you like to sing?" Ms. Callas replied, "The arias from *Iphigénie*, Maestro."[185]

• Joan Oliver Goldsmith, a volunteer singer in a Minnesota chorus, remembers that Christopher Seaman served as guest conductor at a time when the chorus was tired because of having to prepare too many works with not enough time or rehearsals. At a rehearsal of Carl Orff's *Carmina Burana*, he looked at the tired faces of the tired members of the overworked chorus and said, "This piece is meant to be fun. Please modify your faces." The members of the chorus laughed and relaxed. Ms. Goldsmith writes, "Laughter. Suddenly, every singer was engaged. So were our smile muscles." Preparing the members of the chorus for the same *Carmina Burana*, choral director Kathy Romey, who was pregnant, wanted and needed a way for the singers to be heard over the orchestra. She told them, "I need more. Focus. A laser beam." She raised her voice and said, "I want to feel *fetal movement*!" Ms. Goldsmith writes, "No one but Kathy in that moment could have made that remark. Ridiculous and effective." By the way, Ms. Goldsmith's mother, who had just turned 75 years old, once asked her, "How did I get to be so *old*?" Ms. Goldsmith replied, "By getting out of bed every morning."[186]

• When young-adult author Richard Peck was in junior high school, he was asked to play the sousaphone in the marching band because he was the only student who was tall enough to play it. Richard readily agreed to play the sousaphone because it was so big that he figured that he would not be able to take it home and therefore he would not have to practice playing it at home on the weekends. Unfortunately for Richard, his band director dropped off the sousaphone at Richard's house every Friday. After Richard had practiced playing it on the weekend, his father took the sousaphone back to Richard's school on Monday morning.[187]

• Leonard Bernstein's father, Sam, resisted Leonard's desire to forge a career in music, preferring instead that Leonard work in the family business. After Leonard became a world-famous composer and conductor, Sam was asked why he had opposed his son's musical ambitions. Sam replied, "How could I know that my son was going to grow up to become Leonard Bernstein?" In contrast, Leonard's mother,

Jennie, supported her son's musical ambitions. When he was a boy who played the piano loudly at home, causing the neighbors to complain, she told the neighbors, "Someday you're going to pay to hear him!"[188]

• Influences are important. When Jimmy Rabbitte, a fictional character in the novel and movie *The Commitments* (Roddy Doyle wrote the novel), formed a soul band, he asked applicants about their influences. If he didn't like their answer, they didn't get in the band — or even a chance to audition. The saxophone player who did get in the band listed his influences as "Clarence Clemons [a tenor saxophonist, aka The Big Man], the Muppets, and the man from *Madness* [a video game]."[189]

**Names and Titles**

• Lee Child created the tough-guy detective character Jack Reacher, hero of a series of detective novels. Where did the name come from? Mr. Child is a tall man, and a little old lady in a supermarket said to him, "You're a nice tall gentleman, so would you reach that can for me?" His wife even said to him, "If this writing thing doesn't work out, you can always be a reacher in a supermarket." These days, Mr. Child smiles when he reads somebody's comments about how he must have chosen the name "Reacher" because of "its forward-going, striving, progressive implications." The name "Jack" came about because when Mr. Child created the character many detectives had "cute or complex first names," he says, explaining, "I wanted to underpin Reacher's blunt and straightforward manner with a blunt and straightforward name. I didn't think the character would have worked with, say, McNaughten Lawrence for a name."[190]

• Some people don't understand punctuation, as author Judy Blume discovered when she found her book *Are You There, God? It Me, Margaret*, in a bookstore in the religion section. She told the bookstore employee, "That book doesn't belong with the Bibles!" The employee said, "Yes, it does." To prove that the book belonged with the Bibles, the bookstore employee read from the copy on the jacket of the book: "Margaret Simon: twelve chats with God." Actually, the copy on the jacket said, "Margaret Simon, twelve, chats with God."[191]

• Danny Thomas starred for 11 seasons (1953-1964) in the TV sitcom *Make Room for Daddy*. His wife came up with the name. Danny was a nightclub comedian who was often away from home, and while he was away, his little daughters, Marlo and Terre, moved into the bedroom with their mother and put their clothes in the dresser. When Danny was coming home for a while, their mother would say, "Make room for Daddy," and Marlo and Terre would move their clothing back to their own rooms.[192]

• Joseph Heller, author of *Catch-22*, once got to meet anti-nuclear weapons activist Bertrand Russell, who was then in his nineties. The meeting did not go well. At Mr. Russell's home in Wales, Mr. Heller introduced himself, and Mr. Russell told him, "Go away, damn you! Never come back here again!" Fortunately, a servant came running after Mr. Heller and explained that Mr. Russell had thought that Mr. Heller was Edward Teller, aka the father of the atomic bomb.[193]

• The young Leonard Bernstein played music loudly both day and night, even when he had roommates to cut down on living expenses. One roommate, Edys Merrill, used to go around with her hands over her ears as she loudly sang, "I hate music — la dee da da dee. But I like to sing: la dee da da dee." Leonard responded by writing a song using those words and sounds — the song was one of a set of five titled *I Hate Music!: A Cycle of Five Kid Songs*. He dedicated the song to her.[194]

• In downtown Manhattan there used to be a sleazy club which ripped off the name of a prominent British comedy troupe by calling itself Monty Python's Flying Circus. After the club went out of business, the real Monty Python started to receive the defunct club's unpaid bills.[195]

**Nobel Prize**

- Richard Feynman once did a good deed for the magician/comedy duo Penn and Teller. He had come to Penn and Teller's show a few times and had enjoyed it, and Penn Jillette and he had eaten dinner together a couple of times and had occasionally talked to each other on the telephone. In his book *God, No!*, Mr. Jillette wrote, "I'd call him to get some quick tutoring on physics so I could pretend to read his books." Once, Penn and Teller needed some dry ice for something they wanted to do on David Letterman's late-night talk show. Mr. Feynman was the only physicist they knew, so Mr. Jillette called him. Mr. Feynman was a theoretical physicist and did not use dry ice, but he said he would try to get hold of a physicist who used dry ice in a laboratory. Sure enough, Mr. Jillette soon received a phone call from a man who taught physics in a community college in Brooklyn. On the phone, the physicist said, "I don't know what kind of practical joke this is, but a Nobel Prize-winning scientist just called me here at the community college, gave me this number, and told me to call Penn of Penn and Teller to help with a Letterman appearance." By the way, when Penn and Teller were starting out, they traveled in a car that had this professionally lettered on the side: ATLANTA CENTERS FOR DISEASE CONTROL AND PREVENTION — SAMPLE TRANSPORT UNIT. Their car was never broken into.[196]
- William Golding, author of *Lord of the Flies*, won the Noble Prize for Literature for the year 1983. The day after he had learned that he had won, he drove his car into a country town and parked his car illegally so he could run into a shop for a couple of minutes. When he left the shop, he discovered that a meter maid had given him a parking ticket. The meter maid pointed to a sign about parking and asked him, "Can't you read?" He then drove around the corner and saw two policemen, whom he asked if he could go to Town Hall and pay his parking fine immediately. One policeman replied, "No, sir, I'm afraid you can't do that." Mr. Golding felt as if the policeman thought of him as one of "those people who are clearly harmless if a bit

silly." The policeman showed him a place on the parking ticket that was marked "name and address of sender" and told him, "You should write your name and address in that place. You make out a cheque for ten pounds, making it payable to the Clerk to the Justices at this address written here. Then you write the same address on the outside of the envelope, stick a sixteen-penny stamp in the top right-hand corner of the envelope, then post it. And may we congratulate you on winning the Nobel Prize for Literature."[197]

**Poetry**

• In Nebraska, Donald Hall read poems to a big audience of high school students. Answering a question about how he got started, he mentioned watching horror movies and reading Edgar Allan Poe. A male student asked him, "Didn't you do it to pick up chicks?"

During a poetry reading, the poet can put on a persona. Mr. Hall wrote that at poetry readings Robert Frost sometimes seemed to be a countrified chicken farmer. Mr. Hall added, "Once I heard him do this routine, then attended the post-reading cocktail party where he ate deviled eggs, sipped martinis, and slaughtered the reputations of Eliot, Williams, Stevens, Moore ...."

Poetry readings are often followed by question-and-answer sessions. At one such session at a Florida college, a student asked him, "How do you reconcile being a poet with being president of Hallmark cards?" The student had done research and discovered that the president of Hallmark cards was named Donald Hall. Mr. Hall pointed out that it is a common name. He wrote, "Once before a reading a man asked me, 'Are you Donald Hall?' 'Yes,' I said. 'So am I,' he said."[198]

• Gwendolyn Brooks, the first black woman to win the Pulitzer Prize, began reading and writing early in life. At age seven, she began writing rhyming couplets, causing her mother to tell her that she would be "as great as Paul Laurence Dunbar," the great African-American poet. To make sure that Gwendolyn had lots of time to read and write, her mother gave her only one chore each day: washing the dishes after the evening meal. A fire once broke out down the street, and Gwendolyn's mother told her about it, thinking that she would like to see it, but Gwendolyn preferred to keep reading. When she won the 1950 Pulitzer Prize for poetry for her book *Annie Allen*, lots of people didn't believe it. She said, "Nobody believed it. Not even my little boy believed it. ... And I guess I didn't believe it either — at first."

When she learned that she won the Pulitzer Prize, the electricity was off in her apartment because she and her husband were having a rough time financially, but her husband was trying hard to get it turned back on. When a photographer from the *Chicago Tribune* arrived, he plugged in his lighting equipment, making her nervous. Fortunately, her husband had managed to get the electricity turned on and the photographer's lights worked.

One person who encouraged her when she was young was author Langston Hughes. Her mother pushed past an usher at a church to get to him and told him, "My daughter *writes*." Mr. Hughes read several of her poems and told her, "You're talented. Keep writing. Some day you'll have a book published." Sixty years afterward, Gwendolyn said, "That did mean a lot to a 16-year-old girl."[199]

• According to Patti Smith, Beat poet "Gregory Corso could enter a room and commit instant mayhem, but he was easy to forgive because he had the equal potential to commit great beauty." Mr. Corso gave Ms. Smith some wisdom when she complained about never being able to finish a poem: "Poets don't finish poems — they abandon them. Don't worry. You'll do OK, kid." And he made his opinion known whenever he attended the readings of poets. When a poet recited something boring, Mr. Corso would shout, "Sh*t! Sh*t! No blood! Get a transfusion!" Ms. Smith made up her mind to not be boring when she recited poetry.[200]

• When he was a kid, author Stanley Kunitz sometimes climbed a cliff with a sheer granite face, testing himself by seeing how high he could go. Once, he got almost to the top but could go no higher.

He also found out that he was too scared to climb back down. After several hours, fire fighters and police officers rescued him with a ladder. Mr. Kunitz says, "I must say my mother didn't appreciate that I was inventing a metaphor for poetry."[201]

# Chapter 5: From Practical Jokes to Work

**Practical Jokes**

- Both Andy Kaufman and his friend Bob Zmuda were masters of the put-on. Once, Andy Kaufman and writer Julie Hecht went into a diner and sat in a booth. A little later, Mr. Zmuda came in and sat at the counter. However, a man walked over to him and told him, "You're sitting in my seat." Mr. Zmuda and the man talked briefly, and then Mr. Zmuda started crying and said, "So I accidentally took a man's seat! How was I supposed to know?" The man and the counterman started to try to comfort him, but Mr. Kaufman then said loudly, "Imagine that, a grown man crying! I'm disgusted. A grown man crying! I'm ashamed for the human race. I'm ashamed to be part of mankind." Mr. Zmuda, still crying, then said, "He thinks he's a big man just because he's got a girl with him." The result of the put-on was that Mr. Kaufman and Ms. Hecht left the diner — at Ms. Hecht's insistence. Shortly afterward, Mr. Zmuda joined them — because of the crying act, the counterman had comped his order. Ms. Hecht was not a big fan of the put-on she had witnessed, but Mr. Kaufman told her, "If you don't like that, I don't know what to tell you. Because doing that is my most favorite hobby in the world."

Later, when Mr. Kaufman was going to appear on *Saturday Night Live*, Mr. Zmuda sat at a desk in a hallway of NBC. He shouted into a phone, "Well, I'm sorry Mr. Kaufman is in the hospital with a heart attack. Andy has to go on live TV; he can't be running to the hospital. ... Where's your *other* son, Mrs. Kaufman?" The looks of the people in the hallway as they listened to this put-on were very satisfying to Mr. Zmuda.

Ms. Hecht once asked Mr. Kaufman if she could leave her tape recorder on until he told her to turn it off. Mr. Kaufman gave her permission, and then he asked Mr. Zmuda, "Have those syphilis sores cleared up yet?"[202]

• On his yacht, Bill Buckley once invited Dick Clurman, an editor at *Time* magazine, to watch a showing of *The Wizard of Oz* emanating from Puerto Rico. Unfortunately, Mr. Buckley had misread the time the movie began, so when he turned the TV set on, the movie had already been on for 30 minutes. Mr. McClure, who had never seen the movie, was disappointed, but Mr. Buckley said, "I wonder if my name cuts any ice down there." Mr. Buckley then telephoned the Puerto Rican TV station, explained who he was, and asked them to please start the movie over again. Mr. McClure, incredulous, watched as the TV screen went blank for a moment, and then the movie started again from the beginning. Actually, this was a practical joke. The movie was on a videocassette — new at the time. Mr. Buckley had only pretended to call the TV station, which was NOT broadcasting the movie. While pretending to talk to the TV station, he had rewound the movie and then started it again.

Mr. Buckley could be prickly. Occasionally, he wrote something in his magazine that caused people to write him and tell him to cancel their subscription to his magazine. Sometimes, he wrote back, "Cancel your own d*mn subscription."[203]

• Comedian George Burns once told movie critic Roger Ebert about a fellow comedian named Joe Jackson who used to wear huge shoes in his stand-up act. After the curtain came down, he would stand so that the audience could see his shoes poking out from under the curtain. However, he would slip out of his shoes and go to the side of the stage. The audience would clap their approval of his act, and at exactly the right time Mr. Jackson would walk out from the side of the stage without his shoes, surprising the audience in the early days although the audience soon grew to know, appreciate, and expect the joke. One day, Mr. Jackson did his act as usual and slipped out of his shoes as usual, but then had a heart attack and died at the side of the stage. The audience, of course, knew the joke, and they applauded and applauded, giving Mr. Jackson the biggest ovation of his life, but he was no longer alive to hear it. When Mr. Burns told this story, some people actually cried. When that happened, Mr. Burns told Mr. Ebert, "I hate to break the news to them that I made it up."[204]

• Hugh Troy was a noted practical joker. He once held a party for his friend Stephen Potter, author of *Gamesmanship*. He invited many guests, and each of them brought a Potter book for Mr. Potter to sign, but all of the books were by other authors who had Potter for their last name. At another of his parties in which an author was the guest of honor, Mr. Troy's guests all brought a copy of the author's book to sign, but when the guests left the party, they left behind piles of the autographed books.[205]

• Scottish singer Kenneth McKellar was the victim of a practical joke by Alec Finlay. During a performance, Mr. McKellar was supposed to stand under an apple tree, pick apples, and put them in a basket. However, he discovered that Mr. Finlay had recently varnished each apple, making it stick to his fingers.[206]

• Comedian Ernie Kovacs, whose personal motto was "Nothing in Moderation," was an original. He once needed to have a fluoroscopic examination, so before the exam he wrote on his chest in aluminum paint these words: "Out to Lunch."[207]

**Prejudice**

• Moe Howard of Three Stooges fame discovered racism against blacks while performing early in his career in Jacksonville, Florida, in 1931. He and an elderly black man were walking toward each other on the sidewalk, and when the black man neared him, the black man jumped into the street. Thinking that the black man had seen a snake or something else that was frightening, Moe jumped into the street, whereupon the black man jumped back on the sidewalk, as did Moe. This jumping into the street and then back onto the sidewalk kept on, and finally Moe grabbed the black man's arm and asked, "What the hell is going on, pop? Why are you leaping up and back like a jumping jack?" The black man said, "Sir, in this city a black man mustn't walk on the same side of the street with a white man." Moe replied, "Mister, this is not my city, but it's my country and I can walk with any man I choose to." He then put his arm around the black man and walked a short distance with him; however, the black man said, "Man, you seem nice, but you're liable to get us killed."

When Moe got to the theater where he and the other Stooges were supposed to perform, the stagehands would not prepare the stage for them and the manager of the theater told the Stooges, "Your baggage and trunks have gone back to the [train] station; here is your music, and salary check. We don't want any n*gger lovers in our theater or in our city, so get movin' before you get in *big* trouble."

Forty years later, Moe met a man who told him, "I've always wanted to apologize for playing you dirty in Jacksonville. I was one of the stagehands who wouldn't hang your scenery for walking with the black man. I had to go along with them or lose my job. Please forgive me." Moe gave him a photograph of the Three Stooges, and the man walked away smiling.[208]

- Amiri Baraka grew up in a racist age, and while he was dating a white woman named Hettie Cohen who later became his wife, they were walking together in Greenwich Village when a number of white people started to jeer at them. Angry, Hettie turned toward them, "ready to fight or preach," as she later wrote, but Amiri, who at the time was named LeRoi Jones, grabbed her arm and told her, "Keep walking. Just keep on walking." Hettie wrote, "It was his tone that made me give in, and only later I realized we might have been hurt, or *killed* — and him more likely." The two worked at a music store called The Record Changer, which was going out of business, and they were looking for other jobs. Hettie once listened as Amiri (LeRoi) pretended on the telephone to be his boss, giving himself (LeRoi) a recommendation. He said to the person on the other end of the telephone, "Yes, I'm well aware that he's a Negro, but he's been a fine employee." Shortly after, he said on the telephone, "He hasn't stolen anything, if that's what you mean. We'd be glad to vouch." His face remained calm as he spoke, but Hettie noticed that his jaw muscles clenched and unclenched as if he were grinding his teeth.[209]

- In 1914, African-American author Langston Hughes was 12 years old. He enrolled in Central School in Lawrence, Kansas. His teacher, who was white, wanted black students to sit in a certain row, separate from white students. Langston made up cards for the black students to put on their desks: "JIM CROW ROW." He was expelled from school, but he was allowed to return when black parents and VIPs spoke up for him. The teacher stopped requiring black students to sit in the Jim Crow row. When Langston was in the first grade in Topeka, Kansas, his mother, Carrie, enrolled him in Harrison Street School, which was all white. The principal would not admit him until Carrie went before the Topeka School Board and won.[210]

**Problem-Solving**

- Comedian Alan Abel was a true original. He knew how to get the things he wanted without having to break the law. For example, on a plane, he wanted a seat without any passengers sitting by him. Therefore, he would put a string in his mouth and let the end hang out. Other passengers would see the string and decide not to sit by him. And if he saw a long line at a bank during the lunch hour, he would buy a lunch to go, stand in line a moment, ask a person to save his place in line, and then go to an empty teller's booth, take out a napkin, his lunch, and a *Wall Street Journal*, and eat lunch. Usually, someone such as a Vice President would see him, not want him to eat lunch there, and take care of his transaction, so he would be out of the bank in five minutes. And if someone rang his doorbell, he would put on his coat before he answered it. That way if it was someone he did not want to talk to, he could say that he was just on his way out. And if he got a telephone call from a person he did not want to talk to, he would say that he had a deadline to meet, and then start barking orders to an imaginary employee: "Henry, don't put that there!" The person on the telephone would hear that he was busy, say goodbye, and hang up.[211]

- Comedian Milton Berle once guest-starred on Marlo Thomas' TV series *That Girl*, and he was a pain in the butt, complaining constantly about everything. Things got so bad that Marlo telephoned her father, the comedian Danny Thomas, to ask for advice. Danny told her, "Ask him to spell words that begin with R." This, of course, makes no sense whatsoever, so Marlo replied, "What? Ask him to spell words that start with R? What are you talking about?" Danny told her, "Just do it." Marlo yelled to Milton, "Hey, Milton, how do you spell *recluse*?" Milton replied, "R-E-C-Q-U-L-S-E," and people laughed. Then Marlo yelled, "How do you spell *remember*?" Milton replied, "R-E-M-M-M-E-M-M-M-B-M-M-E-R-M," and everybody laughed. As soon as Milton got a few laughs, he stopped complaining. Marlo says, "Milton just wanted to feel comfortable. And he felt comfortable when people were laughing. Now he could go to work."[212]

- George Burns and Gracie Allen raised a couple of children with the help of servants. One evening, they returned home and discovered that all of the pictures had been cut out of the dictionary with scissors. George asked his son, Ronnie, where his sister had hidden the scissors. Ron didn't know. Then George asked his daughter, Sandy, where her brother had hidden the scissors. She replied that he had hidden them in a drawer. George was happy that his detective work was successful, and he gave Ronnie a very light punishment. For years afterward he told the story of how his detective work had uncovered the culprit until his now grown-up daughter said to him, "Please don't tell the scissors story tonight, Dad." George asked, "Why not, sweetheart?" Sandy replied, "The reason I knew where they were is that I was the one who cut out the pictures."[213]

- Early in his career, comedian Red Skelton joined a troupe of actors and played straight roles. For example, he played many roles in a play version of *Uncle Tom's Cabin*. He once ran into a problem when he played a slave escaping across a frozen river: The bloodhounds would not chase him. To solve the problem, Red filled his pockets with raw beef liver. The bloodhounds did chase him, and they ripped his clothing to get at the raw beef liver. Red was left with permanent scars.[214]

**Profanity**

• The boys in Sister Margaret Anne's 5th-grade class at the Catholic school got into trouble one day when one of the girl students reported to the principal that the boys were using swear words on the playground. Therefore, Sister Margaret Anne made her students write down all the swear words they knew before they were allowed to leave the classroom. The girls listed words such as "hell" and "damn" and got to go home, but when a boy wrote down only "hell" and "damn," Sister Margaret Anne told him, "Go back to your seat." She knew that the boy had not written all the swear words he knew.

One of the boys in the class was Jon Scieszka, who would later be an author of books for young people. He — and the other boys in the class — knew a lot of swear words, but they did not want to write them on a piece of paper that a nun would read. What to do? Jon wrote down "hell" and "damn," like the other students. Then he wrote down "stupid," "doofus," "butt," and "goober." At that time, he had an inspiration: He could add the word "head" to the words he already had and make the list longer. Therefore, he wrote down "stupidhead," "doofushead," "butthead," and "gooberhead." Then he realized that he could combine words to make up new words that would not be any worse than the words that he had already listed. Therefore, he wrote, "stupidhell," "gooberbutt," doofusdamn," and "hellbutt." This made an impressively long list of swear words. He gave it to Sister Margaret Anne, who looked it over, and to Jon's immense relief, said, "That will be enough." For a while, Jon worried that a vengeful God might drive a bus over him, but God is merciful and let Jon get safely home.[215]

- Opera singer Nellie Melba lived in the infancy of recording. She once tried recording, but as she listened to the screeching, scratchy result, she said to herself, "Never again. Don't tell me I sing like that, or I shall go away and live on a desert island, out of sheer pity for the unfortunate people who have to listen to me." That recording was destroyed. Of course, the process of recording improved, and she later made some recordings with the Victor Talking Machine Company. Also of course, a mishap occasionally occurred. For example, she had just about finished making an excellent recording when she tripped backwards over a chair and said, "Damn!" Ms. Melba wrote in her autobiography, *Melodies and Memories*, "That 'damn,' when the record was played over, came out with a terrible clarity, making me feel much as a sinner must on the Day of Judgment."

Ms. Melba once watched *Walkyrie* at Covent Garden. In the seat behind her was Alfred de Rothschild. Ms. Melba was completely absorbed in the opera, but then she heard a sound that was definitely not from the opera — Alfred de Rothschild was snoring. He woke up and asked, "What key is it?" Ms. Melba replied that he had been snoring in a different key.[216]

- The United States Post Office engaged in censorship in the late 1950s, refusing to deliver certain publications it objected to. In 1959, Senator Gale McGee was asked about his plans for this session of Congress. He answered, "I'm going to introduce a resolution to have the Postmaster General stop reading dirty books and deliver the mail."[217]

**Public Speaking**

- The year after newspaperman Heywood Broun died in 1939, many of his friends held a Heywood Broun Memorial meeting for him at the Newspaper Guild of New York at Manhattan Center. Many famous people spoke and told anecdotes about him.

Theodore S. Kenyon knew him for many years. He remembered that Heywood did well in academic subjects that interested him and not at all well in academic subjects that did not interest him. Foreign languages did not interest him. He did so badly in German that his teacher threw an inkwell at him (in the days before ball-point pens, people dipped their pens into inkwells filled with ink), and he did so badly in French that he did not graduate from Harvard.

One of his personal idiosyncrasies was a lack of interest in packing well. Slovenly in his attire (he wore a uniform so badly as a war correspondent during World War I that General John Joseph Pershing asked him whether he had fallen down), his method of packing was to throw stuff into a suitcase until it was full and then to stand on the stuff to pack it down so he could throw in more stuff.

How famous were the people at the memorial meeting? Mr. Kenyon's daughter looked over the names of the people who would speak and then she told her father, "Why, Daddy, you're the only one in the whole lot that I never heard of!" (This is probably a bit of an exaggeration; after all, Mr. Broun's favorite cabdriver and waiter were among the speakers.)[218]

• Comedian Don Knotts was once requested to emcee a dinner for fellow comedian Bob Hope. At first, Mr. Knotts was reluctant to emcee the dinner because he didn't think he was that good at emceeing, but when the very persuasive promoter of the dinner told him that Mr. Hope had specifically requested that Mr. Knotts be the emcee, he agreed. However, when he arrived at the dinner, Mr. Hope greeted him and then asked, "Hi, Don. What are you doing here?"[219]

• When Mark Twain was scheduled to speak at a small town, he would often enter a store and ask if people knew about his lecture being scheduled that night. Once he entered a grocery store and asked if there was anything special going on that evening. The grocer replied, "I think there's a lecture tonight — I've been selling eggs all day."[220]

**Television**

• Joan Davis, star of the 1950s TV sitcom *I Married Joan*, was a true comedian who, co-star Jim Backus says, "knew every joke ever written." Like many comedians, she sometimes engaged in risqué humor. Her show involved a lot of physical comedy, and a guest star once said that for one stunt he was going to need a cup, aka athletic supporter. Joan eyed him and said, "From what I can see, all you'll need is a demitasse [small cup]." For one scene in the sitcom, a turtle was supposed to move around and evade her, but no matter what she and the animal trainer did, the turtle would not move. Finally, Joan gave up, but she told the turtle, "You SOB, you'll never work for me again."[221]

• Comedian George Lindsey auditioned for the part of Gomer Pyle on *The Andy Griffith Show*, but Jim Nabors got the part. Mr. Lindsey was very disappointed, and at home, when he watched the episode introducing Gomer, he became so angry that he kicked in the screen of the TV. Fortunately, Mr. Nabors left to do the spin-off series *Gomer Pyle, U.S.M.C.*, and Mr. Lindsey started appearing on *The Andy Griffith Show* as Gomer's cousin, Goober Pyle. Mr. Lindsey did much good in his life as a supporter of the Special Olympic and people with learning disabilities.[222]

• Children's fantasy author Tamora Pierce sets herself a quota of pages to write each day. As deadlines grow nearer, she must write more pages. If she doesn't reach her quota of pages, she won't allow herself to watch TV that day. (Most evenings, she watches TV.)[223]

• Comedian Bill Hicks could be pretty hard-hitting. When he heard that the Supreme Court had defined pornography as being something that has "no artistic merit and causes sexual thought," he remarked, "Sounds like every commercial on television."[224]

**Timing**

• Bob Newhart was known for his comic delivery, which is deadpan, frequently slow, and occasionally stuttering. Once, a director tried to make him speed up his delivery, but Mr. Newhart told him, "This stutter built me a house in Bel-Air. Don't mess with it." On another occasion, as Mr. Newhart was traveling on an airplane, he listened to some comedy tracks on his headset, where he heard one of his "Button-Down" stand-up routines. Unfortunately, the track had been edited to take out all his pauses — which completely threw off the timing. Mr. Newhart told his friend Betty White that he felt like standing up in the aisle, apologizing to the audience, and then performing the routine the way it should be performed.[225]

• Buddy Hackett once said to Johnny Carson, "Ask me what the secret of comedy is." Johnny said, "What's the secret of — " and Buddy yelled in his face, "TIMING!" In his house, Johnny kept a throw pillow that had this embroidered on it: "It's All in the Timing."[226]

**Valentine's Day**

• When Katherine Patterson, the author of *Bridge to Terebithia*, was a very young girl, she was very shy and so found it difficult to make friends. On Valentine's Day, she returned home very sad because she had not gotten any Valentines. Her mother never forgot Katherine's sadness, and years later, after Katherine was a successful author, she asked her why she had never written about not getting any Valentines. Katherine replied, "But, mother, all my stories are about the time I didn't get any Valentines."[227]

**Vaudeville**

• Comedian Fred Allen spent years entertaining people in vaudeville, and as you would expect, he had many stories to tell. One of the big-time acts in vaudeville was Nelson's Cats and Rats, in which these natural enemies performed tricks. In Chicago, Illinois, Fanny Brice screamed in her dressing room. The stage manager asked, "What's wrong, Miss Brice?" She said, "A rat! There's a big rat in my dressing room!" The stage manager called for Nelson, who caught the rat. A few weeks later, comedian Fred Allen performed in the same theater as Nelson's Cats and Rats, and he asked Nelson what had become of the rat that had been in Fanny Brice's dressing room. Nelson replied, "In the next show, watch the finish of my act." My Allen watched the finish, in which a big rat walked across a tiny platform while holding an American flag in its mouth. After the show, Nelson told Mr. Allen, "That is the rat."

Another act was Raymonde, a female impersonator. Raymonde did his entire act as a woman, and at the end, when the audience applauded, he took off his wig and showed the audience a male haircut. The audience would be amazed to discover that Raymonde was a man, and they would applaud harder. Then Raymonde would take off the male wig and reveal long blonde feminine hair that tumbled down. The audience would applaud even harder, and Raymonde would take off that wig, revealing his real male haircut and then walk off stage in the manner of a very masculine truck driver as the audience applauded hardest of all.

Mishaps and odd things, of course, occurred in the theater and in theatrical life. The manager of one vaudeville theater in Sherbrooke, Ontario, Canada, also had a business that sold raincoats. He once tried to convince the vaudevillians working in his theater to take their pay in raincoats rather than money.

In Lancaster, Pennsylvania, Mr. Allen performed in a small theater in a building that had a bowling alley upstairs. Mr. Allen told a joke, only to have the punch line drowned out by the noise of a strike upstairs.

In a theater in Bayonne, New Jersey, during Mr. Allen's act, a cat lay down in an aisle and delivered a litter of kittens. Mr. Allen said, "I thought my act was a monologue, not a catalogue."

In the Jefferson Theatre on Fourteenth Street in New York City, Mr. Allen was mystified by a noise that occurred at 30-second intervals during his comic monologue: a clunk. Eventually, he discovered that a member of the audience was shucking oysters and then dropping the shells into a wooden bucket: clunk ... clunk ... clunk.

Comedian Ted Healey — whom the Three Stooges used to work for — once had a large bill at the Lincoln Hotel in New York City and no way to pay it. He was unable to get his trunk out of his room because he had no money to pay his bill, so he ordered the Three Stooges to go to his room. Each Stooge and Mr. Healey put on three suits of clothing and an overcoat and walked out of the hotel, leaving behind an empty trunk and a large bill.[228]

• W.C. Fields enjoyed taking money from the movie studios that employed him. Whenever he was shown a script, he would say that it needed punching up — which he was willing to do for $50,000. The movie studio would pay the money, and Mr. Fields would punch up the script by inserting one of his old vaudeville routines, even if it had nothing to do with the plot.[229]

**War**

• Comedian Red Skelton served as a private during World War II. On leave, he stopped to see Louis B. Mayer, head of Metro-Goldwyn-Mayer, who asked, "How is Army life?" Red replied, "I don't like it at all." Mr. Meyer asked, "Don't you get fed well?" Red replied, "Three square meals a day." Mr. Meyer asked, "You have a roof over your head?" Red replied, "We always have a roof over our head. Barracks. Tents. Whatever. It never rains on us when we are sleeping." Mr. Meyer asked, "Clothing?" Red replied, "Wool clothing in the winter. Nice cottons in the summer. We have nice uniforms." Mr. Meyer asked, "What is it about the Army you don't like?" Red replied, "Bullets, Mr. Meyer."[230]

• Bob Hope spent decades entertaining the troops. They liked his comedy, and they also liked the pretty female entertainers he brought with him. For some shows in Korea (and no doubt in other countries), newspaper columnist Irv Kupcinet remembers that Mr. Hope brought the beautiful and Irish Erin O'Brien. When she walked out onstage, a GI shouted, "My name is Tom Coughlin." Ms. O'Brien said, "A fine Irish boy like you deserves a kiss," and she kissed him. Immediately, the other GIs started shouting, "My name is O'Callahan … My name is Shanahan … My name is Kelly."[231]

**Wits**

• Joseph Epstein has a reputation as a wit that he thinks he does not deserve. Wits, of course, are quick to come up with witty sayings, and all too often, Mr. Epstein thinks up witty sayings after it is too late to say them. For example, while teaching he asked a student named Jonathan Stern to describe the character Gilbert Osmond, who is in Henry James's novel *The Portrait of a Lady*. Mr. Stern called the character "an asshole." Mr. Epstein was apparently the only person in the classroom who was shocked. He said that each student was allowed one use of curse words per course and the student had used up his allotment for the semester. Mr. Epstein wrote, "Only later, leaving class, actually walking down the stairs, did it occur to me that what I should have said was, 'I'm pleased, Mr. Stern, that I didn't ask you to describe Oedipus Rex.'" Mr. Epstein's children can be funny. He once made Italian meat sauce and his children joked that the movie this reminded them of was Absorba the Grease, otherwise known as *Zorba the Greek*.[232]

• Dorothy Parker was fired from her job as a drama critic at *Vanity Fair* because she panned the plays of three very powerful men: Dillingham, Ziegfeld, and Belasco. In solidarity with her, Robert Sherwood and Robert Benchley quit. Ms. Parker said, "It was the greatest act of friendship I'd known." They all went to work for *Life*, where she and Mr. Benchley shared an office of which she famously observed, "He and I had an office so tiny that an inch smaller and it would have been adultery." As you would expect, Ms. Parker was a good interviewee. Marion Capron of *The Paris Review* asked her, "What, then, would you say is the source of most of your work?" Ms. Parker replied, "Need of money, dear." Ms. Parker at first wrote in longhand, although she later used a typewriter: "I wrote in longhand at first, but I've lost it. I use two fingers on the typewriter. [...] I know so little about the typewriter that once I bought a new one because I couldn't change the ribbon on the one I had."[233]

- Frequently, an actor can get free merchandise or services by mentioning a manufacturer or business on a TV show. After Groucho Marx mentioned Arthur Murray, who taught dancing, on *You Bet Your Life*, he wrote Mr. Murray and asked to be sent "a medium-sized dancing girl, about 5'2", with the customary measurements. I am not particular as to what kind of hair she has, as long as she has hair." Groucho once received a business letter in which a banking firm wrote to ask what assistance they could give him. Groucho wrote back, "Frankly, the best assistance you could give me is to steal some money from the account of one of your richer clients and credit it to mine."[234]
- Jazz alto saxophonist Paul Desmond likes plays on words. After learning about the sale of a Rembrandt for an amazing amount of money, Mr. Desmond created this joke: Buster Keaton owned a very expensive home in Beverly Hills, but having decided to economize, he wanted to sell the mansion. Aristotle Onassis, a very rich Greek, had the money to buy the mansion, and he decided to look at it. A newspaper reporter happened to be at hand, and he snapped a photograph of Mr. Onassis on the grounds. The photograph appeared in the next day's newspaper with this caption: "Aristotle Contemplating the Home of Buster."[235]
- George Bernard Shaw was present at the opening day of his play *Arms and the Man*. At the final curtain, the applause was overwhelming and there were cries of "Author! Author!" However, when Mr. Shaw appeared on stage to take his bow, one person could be heard hissing amidst the cheers. Mr. Shaw turned in the direction of the hissing, raised his hand for silence, and then told the dissenter, "I agree with you, sir, but what can we two do against so many?" A society lady once sent her card to Mr. Shaw. The card said that she would be "at home from 4:30 p.m. to 6:30 p.m. on Thursday next." Mr. Shaw sent the card back with this message written on it: "So will Mr. Shaw."[236]

- While playing poker in Hollywood, Groucho Marx and George S. Kaufman spoke up simultaneously and made the same witticism. Groucho said, "Before you came here, I used to be a big man around this town. But now people will say, 'Did you hear what George S. Kaufman and Groucho Marx said?'"[237]

**Work**

- Dominic Holden, a writer for the Seattle, Washington, newspaper *The Stranger*, used to work as a waiter. Four young Russians came into the restaurant where he worked and ordered something sweet and shots of room-temperature vodka. Mr. Holden happily served them their order, but trouble arose. The four young Russians had apparently drunk too much, and their table was covered with brown butcher paper on which a lit candle was sitting. The Russians used the candle to set on fire the brown butcher paper, and smoke began to fill the restaurant. Mr. Holden cheerily told them to put out the fire, and they obeyed, but soon they again set the paper on fire. This time, Mr. Holden ordered them more firmly to put out the fire. When the restaurant closed, the Russians paid their $75 tab and had only $1.52 in coins to leave as a tip. This tip was not satisfactory to Mr. Holden, who told them that they MUST leave a bigger tip. The Russians said that they had no more money, but Mr. Holden told them, "Go to the cash machine and get me a real tip." How much is a real tip? On a $75 tab, at least $10. The Russians got the money and left a $10 tip, but the next morning they showed up at the restaurant and complained to the manager, who fired Mr. Holden, who says, "Fair of him to fire me, but I'd do it again."

Other *Stranger* staff worked in food places. For example, writer Lindy West worked in the Backdoor Bakery, kind of. Actually, she worked a few hours for free as she auditioned for the job, which she did not stay around to get. The bosses put her on the orange juicer — for hours. Ms. West says, "The Backdoor Bakery went through many, many gallons of fresh-squeezed orange juice every day. Math fact: The number of oranges required to make one gallon of fresh-squeezed orange juice is eleventy grillion. Backdoor Bakery fact: All of those oranges were juiced BY HAND. SPECIFICALLY, MY F**KING HAND. There was an 'electric' juicer, but it only 'worked' if you leaned into it mightily at an arm-torquing angle. I juiced and juiced and juiced for hours. I sweated, I groaned, my limbs cramped." Eventually, Ms. West found herself alone with an employee who whispered to her, "Get out. Run. Don't work here. Run. Get OUT." She did.

Another *Stranger* writer, David Schmader, served a regular customer who was known as "Total Bitch" — an affectionate nickname. In fact, she used the term when Mr. Schmader first served her. Mr. Schmader remembers that she said to him, without making eye contact, "I'm a total bitch. But I'm a stud tipper. Now bring me my sh*t." Her sh*t was a plate of scrambled eggs and a coffee with five creams, and she expected to be served that every time she entered the restaurant without anyone asking her what she wanted. She worked as a bartender at a strip club, and after working her shift, all she wanted was her eggs and her coffee — no chitchat. Mr. Schmader says, "I loved her honesty. Serving her was an honor. Her bill always came to four dollars and some change. She always left a five-dollar tip."[238]

• Early in his career as a stand-up comedian, Bill Cosby got his best — to that time — gig ever: He was hired to perform at Mr. Kelly's, a big-time nightclub in Chicago. Unfortunately, he psyched himself out and convinced himself that he was not funny enough to be a success at such a big-time nightclub. The result, of course, is that he bombed big time at the big-time nightclub. Even worse, he was supposed to do another show that night, and he was convinced that he would bomb again.

One of Mr. Kelly's owners was George Marienthal, who visited Mr. Cosby in his dressing room after he bombed. Mr. Cosby told him, "Mr. Marienthal, I am very, very sorry for what happened, and I am very sorry for what I did tonight. I refuse to accept any pay from you. [...]

And as soon as I get the money I will pay you back for the plane trip, the hotel room, and everything else, but I will not be going out to do the second show. I am going back to Temple University. [...] I am going to play football, and I am going to graduate from college and get my master's and my doctorate."

Mr. Marienthal agreed to everything he had heard, but he added, "When you get back to your hotel, will you tell Bill Cosby to come back here and do the second show and to never send you again, because you, sir, you are *not* funny. Bill Cosby is very, very funny. I don't know why he sent you. Probably because he was afraid. Who knows what happens in the minds of entertainers? But, sir, *you* get out of here and you bring Bill Cosby — you *send* Bill Cosby. Do whatever, but Bill Cosby *has* to come back here and do the second show."

Mr. Cosby did return to do the second show, and the announcer announced him as "Bill Cosby." That's it. Just "Bill Cosby." For the first show, the announcer had announced him as "one of the fastest-rising young comedians." Mr. Cosby went onstage and complained to the announcer about how he had just been introduced. He explained to the audience that for the first show he had been introduced as "one of the fastest-rising young comedians" and now he was not. And he asked the announcer to explain why he had not given him a better introduction. The announcer explained on the loudspeaker, "That's because I saw the first show." The audience laughed, and Bill Cosby — the real Bill Cosby — was funny that night.

After the second show, Mr. Marienthal visited him in his dressing room and said, "Bill, wonderful show. Who was that horrible fellow you sent for the first show?" Mr. Cosby replied, "Mr. Marienthal, I hope never to send him out on the stage again." Mr. Marienthal then said, "If you do, you ought to really, before you even think about it, realize that there are some people out there who want to laugh."

Another person who got good advice was Kathryn Stockett, who wrote the novel *The Help*, which was a major success both as a book and as a movie. The book was rejected — and rewritten — many times before an agent read it and agreed to try to sell it to a publisher. Ms. Stockett remembers meeting published authors who advised her, "Just keep at it. I received fourteen rejections before I finally got an agent. *Fourteen!* How many have you gotten?" Unfortunately, the answer was 55 — and counting. She did not give up. Even while pregnant in the hospital, she was working on doing research to incorporate in her book to make it better. A nurse told her, "Put the book down, you nut job — you're *crowning*!" Finally, after 60 rejections and five years of writing and rewriting, she got an agent: Susan Ramer. Three weeks later, Ms. Ramer sold *The Help*.[239]

• Entertainers in show business can be big, and then, later, they can be not so big. Marty Allen and Steve Rossi were big: They appeared on *The Ed Sullivan Show* 44 times. In the 1990s, Penn Jillette and Teller of Penn and Teller fame were headlining at Trump Plaza in Atlantic City, New Jersey. Being headliners, they were in the big room — the room with the theater where the audience plays attention to the performers. Penn and Teller would open the next night, and this night Penn got a call from Mr. Rossi inviting him and Teller to see Allen and Rossi perform their act in a lounge. Lounges are places in the open. They don't have walls, and unless the entertainers are in a band that makes a lot of sound, it can be difficult to get people to pay attention to you. In addition, the noise that can be heard coming from the casino can be a big distraction. Allen and Rossi were funny; they were committed to putting on a good show; they were great. But this was not the high point of their careers, and few people were present to pay attention to them, although Penn and Teller and a few others were enjoying the act. In a break between bits, Teller, who had been intently watching and laughing at the comedy, looked around the room and noticed the few people who were present and the noise that was coming from the casino. Penn leaned over to him and said, quietly, "You know, this is us in a very few years." Teller looked around again, smiled, and replied, "I am so OK with that." Penn, happy with the reply, cried a little.[240]

- Respect other people so that they can respect you. A guest conductor came to Minnesota and requested a chorus to sing for free. Lots of requests went out. Unfortunately, the guest conductor had been to this area before and had treated many members of many choruses — and the choruses as a whole — with contempt. According to Joan Oliver Goldsmith, a volunteer singer in a Minnesota chorus, "He got inexperienced kids who were impressed by his name."

By the way, Ms. Goldsmith once talked to a friend of hers — a business consultant who also practices Zen — about clients he will never work for again, and he said, "By the time I was forty, I had developed one of the great philosophies of my life: Avoid *ssholes."

And a French hornist once told her that if a symphony orchestra respects a guest conductor, the musicians will keep their music stands low during rehearsal so that they can clearly see the conductor, but if the musicians do not respect the conductor, the music stands will be high and the musicians will conduct themselves by ear.[241]

- M.F.K. Fisher began writing because a man was reading an old book about Elizabeth recipes in a public library. When he left the book on a table, she looked at it because she liked its smell and began reading it. She said, "Later I wrote about those recipes simply to amuse my husband and our friends, just as to this day I write books for myself." She did write well. She wrote that "a well-made dry Martini or Gibson, correctly chilled and nicely served, has been more often my true friend than any two-legged creature."

Her feminism sometimes showed in her writing. She and her first husband "sweated out the Depression" by doing such things as cleaning other people's houses. She remembers, "It annoyed the hell out of me because he got 50 cents an hour and I only got 35 cents because I was a woman." Selling her first piece of writing was a joy. She got $10 for the essay and $15 for an illustration that she created to go with the essay.

She remembers, "I thought — am I a writer or am I going to be a sort of mediocre illustrator for the rest of my life?"[242]

- Early in its history, an online book seller whose name rhymes with Bamazon lacked money and inventory space. Of course, it needed to order books, but book distributors required that each order contain at least ten books, and Rhymes-with-Bamazon often needed only one book. Rhymes-with-Bamazon found a way to receive one book in an order. It would order a copy of the book it needed, and then add to the order nine copies of an obscure book on lichens that was always out of stock.

Early employees worked long hours. One employee spent eight months getting up, biking to work, working, and then biking back home and going to sleep. He completely forgot about his blue station wagon and the city law requiring it to be moved occasionally. After eight months, the employee had time to look at his mail — anything that wasn't a bill he had put in a pile. He found several parking tickets, a notice telling him that his car had been moved, a few notices from the towing company, and finally a notice that his car had been auctioned off.[243]

- As a boy, poet Robert Frost found a job at a shoe factory in Salem, Massachusetts; however, he discovered that he did not enjoy the work, which paid $1.50 a day and was dangerous. His job was to use a machine to cut leather patterns; a previous employee, a boy, had lost a finger to the cutting machine while working at the same job. Robert resorted to creative thinking to get out of the job. He did not want to admit that he disliked the work, so he lied and told his very religious mother that he was subjected to profanity that other employees used incessantly. She insisted that he quit the job.

An older Robert once rejected a deal proposed to him by his paternal grandfather, who had money. His grandfather offered to support Robert for a year as he wrote poetry; however, if Robert were not a successful poet at the end of the year, he would give up poetry and get a real job. Robert rejected the offer because he realized that becoming a successful poet takes time — he figured that he needed at least 20 years.[244]

• As of April 2010, Stuart Woods had written 26 consecutive *New York Times* bestsellers, 18 of which were crime novels featuring crime-solver Stone Barrington. Mr. Woods works hard, publishing three books a year. Why does he work so hard? He explains, "It's simple, really. I learned a long time ago that, unless you give a publisher a manuscript, he won't give you any money. I'm not rich. I still have to work for a living." At age 16, he was encouraged to be a writer. He read a humorous article about men's fashion in an Atlanta, GA newspaper, and then he wrote the author, saying that he thought that women's fashion was funnier. The author of the article, a woman, wrote back, "I don't know who you are, but you should be a writer." Mr. Woods says, "Since that was secretly what I wanted to do anyway, that was an enormous amount of encouragement. She was the first person who ever encouraged me to think of myself as a writer, the first person who made me think that I could actually do it."[245]

• One of the stories told about Kurt Vonnegut is how he quit his job writing for *Sports Illustrated*. He was assigned to write a story about a horse that jumped over a fence during a race and tried to run away. Supposedly, Mr. Vonnegut stared for hours at a blank sheet of paper, and then he wrote "The horse jumped over the f**king fence" and quit. Later, as a famous author, he made a cameo in the movie *Back to School*. He played himself, and the character played by Rodney Dangerfield hired him to write a term paper on the novels of Kurt Vonnegut. After Mr. Dangerfield handed in the paper and the professor read it, the professor recognized that the paper was plagiarized and added, "Whoever did write this doesn't know the first thing about Kurt Vonnegut."[246]

• Neil Gaiman, who wrote *Good Omens: The Nice and Accurate Prophecies of Agnes Nutter, Witch* with Terry Pratchett, says about his co-author, "Terry is that rarity, the kind of author who likes Writing, not Having Written, or Being an Author, but the actual sitting there and making things up in front of a screen." Mr. Pratchett was working as a press officer while he wrote his first novel, and each night he wrote 400 words. He needed to write 300 words to finish his first novel, and after he had written the 300 words, he put another sheet of paper in his typewriter (in the days before screens) and wrote 100 words of his second novel.[247]

• Larry David, known especially for his work on *Seinfeld* and *Curb Your Enthusiasm*, used to be a stand-up comedian. The good news is that he was known as a "comedian's comedian." The bad news, he says, is that the meaning of the phrase is this: "I sucked." As a stand-up comedian, he used to chastise the audience for doing such things as talking during his act. Also, on one occasion, he walked up to the microphone and looked at the audience, and then he said, "Ah, never mind," and left the stage.[248]

• On 10 July 2011 the British tabloid *News of the World* ceased publication, the result of a scandal involving reporters illegally tapping telephones. As a result of the scandal, many businesses ceased advertising in *News of the World*. The final crossword puzzle in *News of the World* contained a hidden message. The answers to four clues were these words: "TOMORROW WE ARE SACKED."[249]

• While trying to establish herself as a stand-up comedian, Joan Rivers worked as talent agent Irvin Arthur's secretary. Of course, very important people called who wanted to talk to Mr. Arthur, but if Joan thought that they could help her establish herself as a stand-up comedian, she would introduce herself and do a comic monologue before allowing them to talk to Mr. Arthur.[250]

# Appendix A: Bibliography

Adamson, Joe. *Tex Avery: King of Cartoons*. New York: Da Capo Press, Inc., 1975.

Adir, Karen. *The Great Clowns of American Television*. Jefferson, NC: McFarland & Company, Inc., 1988.

Aldrich, Jr., Nelson W., editor. *George Being George*. New York: Random House, 2008.

Allen, Fred. *Much Ado About Me*. Boston, Massachusetts, and Toronto, Ontario, Canada: Little, Brown and Company, 1956.

Axelrod-Contrada, Joan. *Isabel Allende*. New York: Marshall Cavendish, 2011.

Backus, Jim and Henny. *Forgive Us Our Digressions*. New York: St. Martin's Press, 1988.

Barbera, Joseph. *My Life in 'toons: From Flatbush to Bedrock in Under a Century*. Atlanta, Georgia: Turner Publishing, Inc., 1994.

Benny, Jack, and His Daughter Joan. *Sunday Nights at Seven: The Jack Benny Story*. New York: Warner Books, Inc., 1990.

Bernotas, Bob. *Amiri Baraka*. New York: Chelsea House Publishers, 1991.

Block, Herbert. *Herblock: A Cartoonist's Life*. New York: Times Books, 1998.

Boerst, William J. *Generous Anger: The Story of George Orwell*. Greensboro, North Carolina: Morgan Reynolds, Inc., 2001.

Boerst, William J. *Isaac Asimov: Writer of the Future*. Greensboro, NC: Morgan Reynolds, Inc., 1999.

Bryce, Ivar. *You Only Live Once: Memories of Ian Fleming*. London: Weidenfeld and Nicolson, 1984.

Cameron, Donald. *Conversations with Canadian Novelists*. Toronto, Canada: Macmillan of Canada, 1973.

Caravantes, Peggy. *Deep Woods: The Story of Robert Frost*. Greensboro, NC: Morgan Reynolds, Publishing, 2006.

Cavett, Dick. *Talk Show: Confrontations, Pointed Commentary, and Off-Screen Secrets*. New York: Henry Holt and Company, 2010.

Clark, Roy. *My Life — In Spite of Myself!* With Marc Eliot. New York: Pocket Books, 1994.

Couric, Katie. *The Best Advice I Ever Got: Lessons from Extraordinary Lives*. New York: Random House, 2011.

Crampton, Nancy, photographer. *Writers*. New York: The Quantuck Lane Press, 2005.

Crow, Bill. *Jazz Anecdotes*. New York: Oxford University Press, 1990.

Drennan, Robert E., editor. *The Algonquin Wits*. New York: The Citadel Press, 1968.

Epstein, Lawrence J. *George Burns: An American Life*. Jefferson, NC, and London: McFarland & Company, Inc., Publishers, 2011.

Farr, Jamie. *Just Farr Fun*. With Robert Blair Kaiser. Clearwater, Florida: Eubanks / Donizetti Inc., 1994.

Flagg, James Montgomery. *Roses and Buckshot*. New York: Van Rees Press, 1946.

Ford, Michael Thomas. *The Little Book of Neuroses*. Los Angeles, CA: Alyson Books, 2001.

Freedman, Carl, editor. *Conversations with Isaac Asimov*. Jackson, Mississippi: University Press of Mississippi, 2005.

Friedman, Kinky. *'Scuse Me While I Whip This Out*. New York: Harper, 2004.

Furniss, Maureen, editor. *Chuck Jones Conversations*. With the assistance of Stormy Gunter. Jackson, Mississippi: University Press of Mississippi, 2005.

Gaiman, Neil, and Terry Pratchett. *Good Omens: The Nice and Accurate Prophecies of Agnes Nutter, Witch*. New York: HarperCollins Publishers, 2006.

Garner, Joe. *Made You Laugh: the Funniest Moments in Radio, Television, Stand-up, and Movie Comedy*. Kansas City, MO: Andrews McMeel Publishing, 2004.

Goldsmith, Joan Oliver. *How Can We Keep from Singing: Music and the Passionate Life*. New York and London: W.W. Norton & Company, 2001.

Green, Amy Boothe, and Howard E. Green. *Remembering Walt: Favorite Memories of Walt Disney*. New York: Disney Editions, 1999.

Hackett, Buddy. *The Truth About Golf and Other Lies*. Garden City, New York: Doubleday and Company, Inc., 1968.

Harris, Joseph. *Rewriting: How to Do Things with Texts*. Logan, Utah: Utah State University Press, 2006.

Heath, Chip, and Dan Heath. *Made to Stick: Why Some Ideas Survive and Others Die*. New York: Random House, 2007.

Hecht, Andrew. *Hollywood Merry-Go-Round*. New York: Grosset and Dunlap, Publishers, 1947.

Hecht, Julie. *Was This Man a Genius? Talks with Andy Kaufman*. New York: Random House, 2001.

Hill, Christine M. *Gwendolyn Brooks: "Poetry is Life Distilled."* Berkeley Hills, NJ: Enslow Publishers, Inc., 2005.

Hope, Bob. With Bob Thomas. *The Road to Hollywood: My Forty-Year Love Affair With the Movies*. Garden City, NY: Doubleday & Company, Inc., 1977.

Howard, Moe. *Moe Howard and the Three Stooges*. Secaucus, NJ: Citadel Press, 1977.

Irving, Gordon, compiler. *The Wit of the Scots*. London: Leslie Frewin Publishers, Inc., 1969.

Jessel, George. *Jessel, Anyone?* Englewood Cliffs, NJ: Prentice-Hall, Inc., 1960.

Jillette, Penn. *God, No! Signs You May Already be an Atheist and Other Magical Tales*. New York: Simon and Schuster, 2011.

Jones, Chuck. *Chuck Redux: Drawing from the Fun Side of Life.* New York: Warner Books, Inc. 1996.

Juno, Andrea, and V. Vale, publishers and editors. *Pranks! Devious Deeds and Mischievous Mirth.* San Francisco, CA: Re/Search Publications, 1987.

King-Smith, Dick. *Chewing the Cud.* New York: Alfred A. Knopf, 2001.

Klaiman, Gloria. *Night and Day: The Double Lives of Artists in America.* Westport, CT: Praeger Publishers, 2001.

Knotts, Don. *Barney Fife and Other Characters I Have Known.* With Robert Metz. New York: Berkley Boulevard Books, 1999.

Kohen, Yael. *We Killed: The Rise of Women in American Comedy.* New York: Farrar, Straus and Giroux, 2012.

Krohn, Katherine. *Stephenie Meyer: Dreaming of* Twilight. Minneapolis, Minnesota: Twenty-First Century Books, 2011.

Krull, Kathleen. *Lives of the Writers: Comedies, Tragedies (And What the Neighbors Thought).* San Diego, California: Harcourt Brace & Company, 1994.

Lazar, David, editor. *Conversations with M.F.K. Fisher.* Jackson, Mississippi: University of Mississippi Press, 1992.

Leonard, Sheldon. *And the Show Goes On: Broadway and Hollywood Adventures.* New York: Limelight, 1994.

Linkletter, Art. *I Wish I'd Said That! My Favorite Ad-Libs of All Time.* Garden City, NY: Doubleday & Co., Inc., 1968.

Littleton, Darryl. *Black Comedians on Black Comedy: How African-Americans Taught Us to Laugh.* New York: Applause Theatre & Cinema Books, 2006.

Loos, Anita. *Kiss Hollywood Goodbye.* New York: Ballantine Books, 1974.

Marcus, Leonard S., compiler and editor. *Funny Business: Conversations with Writers of Comedy.* Somerset, MA: Candlewick Press, 2009.

Marcus, Leonard S., compiler and editor. *The Wand in the Word: Conversations with Writers of Fantasy*. Cambridge, MA: Candlewick Press, 2006.

Marx, Arthur. *Red Skelton*. New York: E.P. Dutton, 1979.

Marx, Maxine. *Growing Up with Chico*. New York: Limelight Editions, 1986.

McMahon, Ed. *Here's Ed: Or, How to be a Second Banana*. As told to Carroll Carroll. New York: G.P. Putnam's Sons, 1976.

Melba, Nellie. *Melodies and Memories*. New York: George H. Doran Company, 1926.

Morgan, David. *Monty Python Speaks*. New York: Avon Books, Inc., 1999.

Nachman, Gerald. *Seriously Funny: The Rebel Comedians of the 1950s and 1960s*. New York: Pantheon Books, 2003.

Newspaper Guild of New York. *Heywood Broun as He Seemed to Us*. New York: Random House, 1940. 50 pp.

Pegg, Robert. *Comical Co-Stars of Television*. Jefferson, NC: McFarland & Company, Inc., Publishers, 2002.

Penn & Teller, *Penn & Teller's How to Play in Traffic*. New York: Boulevard Books, 1997.

Penzler, Otto, editor. *The Lineup*. New York: Little, Brown and Company, 2009.

Peterson, T.F. *Nightwork: A History of Hacks and Pranks at MIT*. Cambridge, Massachusetts: MIT Press, 2011.

Provenza, Paul, and Dan Dion. *¡Satiristas!: Comedians, Contrarians, Raconteurs & Vulgarians*. New York: HarperCollins Publishers, 2010.

Pryor, Rain. *Jokes My Father Never Taught Me: Life, Love, and Loss with Richard Pryor*. With Cathy Crimmins. New York: HarperCollins Publishers, 2006.

Reef, Catherine. *Ernest Hemingway: A Writer's Life*. Boston, MA: Clarion Books, 2009.

Reef, Catherine. *Walt Whitman*. New York: Clarion Books, 1995.

Rhynes, Martha E. *Gwendolyn Brooks: Poet from Chicago*. Greensboro, NC: Morgan Reynolds Publishing, Inc., 2003.

Rhynes, Martha E. *I, Too, Sing America: The Story of Langston Hughes*. Greensboro, North Carolina: Morgan Reynolds Publishing, Inc., 2002.

Rickles, Don. *Rickles' Book*. With David Ritz. New York: Simon & Schuster, 2007.

Robbins, Jhan. *Inka Dinka Doo: The Life of Jimmy Durante*. New York: Paragon House, 1991.

Rosen, Michael J., editor. *Horse People: Writers and artists on the Horses They Love*. New York: Workman Publishing Company, Inc., 1998.

Rosten, Leo. *People I Have Loved, Known or Admired*. New York: McGraw-Hill Book Company, 1970.

Rutkowska, Wanda. *Famous People in Anecdotes*. Warszawa: Wydawnictwa Szkolne i Pedagogiczne, 1977.

Sapet, Kerrily. *Rhythm and Folklore: The Story of Zora Neale Hurston*. Greensboro, North Carolina: Morgan Reynolds Publishing, Inc., 2009.

Schochet, Stephen. *Hollywood Stories: Short, Entertaining Anecdotes About the Stars and Legends of the Movies!* Los Angeles, CA: Hollywood Stories Publishing, 2010.

Schwarzkopf, Elisabeth. *On and Off the Record: A Memoir of Walter Legge*. New York: Charles Scribner's Sons, 1982.

Scieszka, Jon. *Knucklehead: Tall Tales and Mostly True Stories About Growing Up Scieszka*. New York: Viking, 2008.

Sellers, Michael, and Gary Morecambe. *Sellers on Sellers*. Additional material by Maxine Ventham. Great Britain: Andre Deutsch, 2000.

Shydner, Ritch, and Mark Schiff, compilers. *I Killed: True Stories of the Road from America's Top Comics*. New York: Crown Publishers, 2006.

Smiles, Roy. *Funny People: My Journey Through Comedy*. London, England: Oberon Books, 2011.

Smith, H. Allen. *How to Write Without Knowing Nothing*. Boston: Little, Brown, and Company, 1961.

Smith, H. Allen. *To Hell in a Handbasket*. Garden City, New York: Doubleday & Company, Inc., 1962.

Smith, Patti. *Just Kids*. New York: HarperCollins Publishers, 2010.

Stefoff, Rebecca. *Herman Melville*. New York: Julian Messner, 1994.

Stefoff, Rebecca. *Stephen King*. New York: Marshall Cavendish, 2011.

Thomas, Danny. *Make Room for Danny*. With Bill Davidson. New York: G.P. Putnam's Sons, 1991.

Thomas, Marlo. *Growing Up Laughing: My Story and the Story of Funny*. Waterville, ME: Thorndike Press, 2010. Large Print.

True, Cynthia. *American Scream: The Bill Hicks Story*. New York: HarperEntertainment, 2002.

Tuttle, Dennis R.. *Life in the Minor Leagues*. Philadelphia, PA: Chelsea House Publishers, 1999.

Vale, V., and Andrea Juno, editors. *Incredibly Strange Music, Vol. 2*. San Francisco, CA: Re/Search Publications, 1994.

Walker, Gerald, editor. *My Most Memorable Christmas*. New York: Pocket Books, Inc., 1963.

Weller, Sam. *Listen to the Echoes: The Ray Bradbury Interviews*. Brooklyn, NY: Melville House, 2010.

White, Betty. *Here We Go Again: My Life in Television*. New York: St. Martin's Press, 1995.

Whitelaw, Nancy. *Nathaniel Hawthorne: American Storyteller.* Greensboro, North Carolina: Morgan Reynolds Publishing, Inc., 1996.

Yungshans, Penelope. *Prize Winners: Ten Writers for Young People.* Greensboro, NC: Morgan Reynolds, Inc., 1995.

Zoglin, Richard. *Comedy at the Edge: How Stand-up in the 1970s Changed America.* New York: Bloomsbury, 2008.

Zolotow, Maurice. *No People Like Show People.* New York: Random House, 1951.

# Appendix B: The Best Letter I Have Ever Received

My Niece Jennifer Jacobs to David Bruce

18 October 2011

Hi, David,

This letter is a couple decades late, but I hope it finds you well.

Everyone knows I love to read. Since having kids, though, I've just been doing light reading, YA novels and things like that. I received a Kindle as a gift last Christmas, and I think it makes it easier to read. I can adjust the font and am able to completely lose myself in the story. I've been very excited rereading the classics I first read when I was a kid. I realized I had missed the language of these books. I also realized that the reason I've already read these books is because of you.

My maternal grandmother babysat me and read to me all day. My mom gave me all her copies of The Boxcar Children, Bobbsey Twins, Nancy Drew and Trixie Belden. You were the one who gave me the classics novels, and I owe you a huge thank you! We weren't able to go very many places when I was growing up, and we lived in the middle of nowhere so I don't know what I would have done without books. I remember getting boxes of books in the mail. If I remember right, you gave me *The Little House on the Prairie* series and *The Chronicles of Narnia*, *A Girl of the Limberlost*, *A Wrinkle in Time* and a ton more. By the time I was a teenager, you had started giving me Charles Dickens, Jules Verne, Jane Austen, John Steinbeck and a ton more. My sophomore year, we read 4 books. I had already read *Huckleberry Finn* and *Of Mice and Men*, thanks to you. The other 2 were *The Scarlet Letter* (didn't really like) and *To Kill a Mockingbird* (need to reread soon – although not on Kindle).

My kids also love to read, which is good because it means I'll keep them. My daughter is 8 now. I've started passing along books to her.

She's read Pippi Longstocking and *Charlotte's Web*. She's working on the Harry Potter books and The Boxcar Children series. She's also reading a set of children classics that my parents had bought for her, *A Little Princess* and *The Wizard of Oz* so far. *Black Beauty* is next. I was a little worried about my son, who's 4. I read him *Beowulf* when he was a baby. I skipped over some of the more graphic parts, but he liked the cadence. He liked to be read to occasionally, but he had to be in the mood. He's recently, though, started bringing us books to read to him so, like I said, I'll keep him. He loves Dr. Seuss.

Anyway, I greatly appreciate all you've done for me over the years. I hope this crazy letter makes some sense. I'm a reader not a writer.
Jennifer
19 October 2011
Hi, David,

I read the e-mail over and I guess it's okay if you want to put it in a book. Feel free to edit. I really was joking when I alluded that I wouldn't keep my kids if they didn't like to read.

I personally wasn't ready for Abigail to read Harry Potter. Those are books any age can enjoy, and there are so many I want her to read while she's still very young. She came home in the 2nd grade and asked if she could watch the movie. Apparently, every kid in her class had seen the movie but her. I told her she has to read the book before she watches the movie so she just went and got my copy, and that was that.

Jennifer

# Appendix C: About the Author

It was a dark and stormy night. Suddenly a cry rang out, and on a hot summer night in 1954, Josephine, wife of Carl Bruce, gave birth to a boy — me. Unfortunately, this young married couple allowed Reuben Saturday, Josephine's brother, to name their first-born. Reuben, aka "The Joker," decided that Bruce was a nice name, so he decided to name me Bruce Bruce. I have gone by my middle name — David — ever since.

Being named Bruce David Bruce hasn't been all bad. Bank tellers remember me very quickly, so I don't often have to show an ID. It can be fun in charades, also. When I was a counselor as a teenager at Camp Echoing Hills in Warsaw, Ohio, a fellow counselor gave the signs for "sounds like" and "two words," then she pointed to a bruise on her leg twice. Bruise Bruise? Oh yeah, Bruce Bruce is the answer!

Uncle Reuben, by the way, gave me a haircut when I was in kindergarten. He cut my hair short and shaved a small bald spot on the back of my head. My mother wouldn't let me go to school until the bald spot grew out again.

Of all my brothers and sisters (six in all), I am the only transplant to Athens, Ohio. I was born in Newark, Ohio, and have lived all around Southeastern Ohio. However, I moved to Athens to go to Ohio University and have never left.

At Ohio U, I never could make up my mind whether to major in English or Philosophy, so I got a bachelor's degree with a double major in both areas, then I added a Master of Arts degree in English and a Master of Arts degree in Philosophy. Yes, I have my MAMA degree.

Currently, and for a long time to come (I eat fruits and veggies), I am spending my retirement writing books such as *Nadia Comaneci: Perfect 10*, *The Funniest People in Comedy*, Homer's *Iliad: A Retelling in Prose*, and *William Shakespeare's* Hamlet: *A Retelling in Prose*.

By the way, my sister Brenda Kennedy writes romances such as *A New Beginning* and *Shattered Dreams*.

# Appendix D: Some Books by David Bruce

**Anecdote Collections**
*250 Anecdotes About Opera*
*250 Anecdotes About Religion*
*250 Anecdotes About Religion: Volume 2*
*250 Music Anecdotes*
*Be a Work of Art: 250 Anecdotes and Stories*
*Boredom is Anti-Life: 250 Anecdotes and Stories*
*The Coolest People in Art: 250 Anecdotes*
*The Coolest People in the Arts: 250 Anecdotes*
*The Coolest People in Books: 250 Anecdotes*
*The Coolest People in Comedy: 250 Anecdotes*
*Create, Then Take a Break: 250 Anecdotes*
*Don't Fear the Reaper: 250 Anecdotes*
*The Funniest People in Art: 250 Anecdotes*
*The Funniest People in Books: 250 Anecdotes*
*The Funniest People in Books, Volume 2: 250 Anecdotes*
*The Funniest People in Books, Volume 3: 250 Anecdotes*
*The Funniest People in Comedy: 250 Anecdotes*
*The Funniest People in Dance: 250 Anecdotes*
*The Funniest People in Families: 250 Anecdotes*
*The Funniest People in Families, Volume 2: 250 Anecdotes*
*The Funniest People in Families, Volume 3: 250 Anecdotes*
*The Funniest People in Families, Volume 4: 250 Anecdotes*
*The Funniest People in Families, Volume 5: 250 Anecdotes*
*The Funniest People in Families, Volume 6: 250 Anecdotes*
*The Funniest People in Movies: 250 Anecdotes*
*The Funniest People in Music: 250 Anecdotes*
*The Funniest People in Music, Volume 2: 250 Anecdotes*
*The Funniest People in Music, Volume 3: 250 Anecdotes*
*The Funniest People in Neighborhoods: 250 Anecdotes*
*The Funniest People in Relationships: 250 Anecdotes*
*The Funniest People in Sports: 250 Anecdotes*
*The Funniest People in Sports, Volume 2: 250 Anecdotes*
*The Funniest People in Television and Radio: 250 Anecdotes*

*The Funniest People in Theater: 250 Anecdotes*
*The Funniest People Who Live Life: 250 Anecdotes*
*The Funniest People Who Live Life, Volume 2: 250 Anecdotes*
*The Kindest People Who Do Good Deeds, Volume 1: 250 Anecdotes*
*The Kindest People Who Do Good Deeds, Volume 2: 250 Anecdotes*
*Maximum Cool: 250 Anecdotes*
*The Most Interesting People in Movies: 250 Anecdotes*
*The Most Interesting People in Politics and History: 250 Anecdotes*
*The Most Interesting People in Politics and History, Volume 2: 250 Anecdotes*
*The Most Interesting People in Politics and History, Volume 3: 250 Anecdotes*
*The Most Interesting People in Religion: 250 Anecdotes*
*The Most Interesting People in Sports: 250 Anecdotes*
*The Most Interesting People Who Live Life: 250 Anecdotes*
*The Most Interesting People Who Live Life, Volume 2: 250 Anecdotes*
*Reality is Fabulous: 250 Anecdotes and Stories*
*Resist Psychic Death: 250 Anecdotes*
*Seize the Day: 250 Anecdotes and Stories*

[1] Source: Gerald Nachman, *Seriously Funny*, pp. 161-163.

[2] Source: Bill Crow, *Jazz Anecdotes*, p. 196.

[3] Source: Dick Cavett, *Talk Show: Confrontations, Pointed Commentary, and Off-Screen Secrets*, p. 193. Also: Don Rickles, *Rickles' Book*, pp. 130-131.

[4] Source: Roger Ebert, "The best damn job in the whole damn world." 3 April 2009
https://www.rogerebert.com/roger-ebert/the-best-damn-job-in-the-whole-damn-world

[5] Source: Marlo Thomas, *Growing Up Laughing: My Story and the Story of Funny*, p. 37.

[6] Source: Dennis McClellan, "Jonathan Winters, comic genius of improvisation, dies at 87." *Los Angeles Times*. 12 April 2013 <http://www.latimes.com/entertainment/news/tv/la-me-winters-20130413,0,379570.story>.

[7] Source: Maxine Marx, *Growing Up with Chico*, p. 116.

[8] Source: Joe Garner, *Made You Laugh*, p. 74.

[9] Source: Roger Ebert, "The best damn job in the whole damn world." 3 April 2009 https://www.rogerebert.com/roger-ebert/the-best-damn-job-in-the-whole-damn-world

[10] Source: Sam Weller, *Listen to the Echoes: The Ray Bradbury Interviews*, pp. 255-256.

[11] Source: Scott Burns, "Count Your Fathers." AssetBuilder. 18 June 2015 http://assetbuilder.com/scott_burns/count_your_fathers

[12] Source: Alexis Petridis, "Ralph Steadman: 'Why was I so vicious? Was I unfair?'" *Guardian*. 28 May 2014 http://www.theguardian.com/film/2014/may/29/ralph-steadman-hunter-s-thompson-gonzo-film>.

[13] Source: Penn & Teller, *Penn & Teller's How to Play in Traffic*, p. 65.

[14] Source: Maxine Marx, *Growing Up with Chico*, p. 97.

[15] Source: David Morgan, *Monty Python Speaks*, pp. 126, 214.

[16] Source: Fred Allen, *Much Ado About Me*, pp. 254-257.

[17] Source: Otto Penzler, editor, *The Lineup*, pp. 286, 288.

[18] Source: John B. Fisher, "Beatrix Potter: Nonpareil." *Great Writers: Their Lives and Works*. Lectures on Cassette. The Teaching Company.

[19] Source: Ellen Urbani, "Review of *Kissing the Mask: Beauty, Understatement and Femininity in Japanese Noh Theater*, by William T. Vollmann." 15 April 2010 http://www.powells.com/review/2010_04_15.html. Originally published in *The Oregonian*. Also: https://en.wikipedia.org/wiki/Seven_Dreams:_A_Book_of_North_American_Landscapes

[20] Source: Paul Provenza and Dan Dion, *¡Satiristas!: Comedians, Contrarians, Raconteurs & Vulgarians*, pp. 66-67.

[21] Source: "James Thurber, The Art of Fiction No. 10": Interviewed by George Plimpton & Max Steele. *The Paris Review*. 1955 http://www.theparisreview.org/interviews/5003/the-art-of-fiction-no-10-james-thurber

[22] Source: John Crace, "Jo Nesbø: 'If Salman Rushdie had been Norwegian, he'd have written a thriller.'" *Guardian* (UK). 28 October 2012 http://www.guardian.co.uk/books/2012/oct/28/jo-nesbo-salman-rushdie-norwegian-thriller

[23] Source: "Kids' Q&A with Daniel Pinkwater." Powells.com. Accessed 31 August 2010 http://www.powells.com/kidsqa/danielpinkwater.html

[24] Source: Rebecca Stefoff, *Herman Melville*, pp. 65-66, 73, 77, 82, 135-136.

[25] Source: Donald Cameron, *Conversations with Canadian Novelists*, Part 1, pp. 3-4, 6-8, 10.

[26] Source: Joan Axelrod-Contrada, *Isabel Allende*, pp. 11, 17-18.

[27] Source: Carl Freedman, editor, *Conversations with Isaac Asimov*, pp. 17-18, 100, 151, 163.

[28] Source: "Ray Bradbury, The Art of Fiction No. 203": Interviewed by Sam Weller. *The Paris Review*. 2010
http://www.theparisreview.org/interviews/6012/the-art-of-fiction-no-203-ray-bradbury>.

[29] Source: Christine M. Hill, *Gwendolyn Brooks: "Poetry is Life Distilled,"* pp. 38-39, 107-108.

[30] Source: Jean Stein, "Interview with *The Paris Review*. Spring 1956 No. 12
http://www.theparisreview.org/interviews/4954/the-art-of-fiction-no-12-william-faulkner

[31] Source: Michael J. Rosen, editor, *Horse People: Writers and artists on the Horses They Love*, pp. 70-73.

[32] Source: Katie Roiphe, "Do Childish People Write Better Children's Books?" *Slate*. 29 March 2012
http://www.slate.com/articles/arts/roiphe/2012/03/the_restless_life_of_margaret_wise_brown_author_of_goodnight_moon_.single.html

[33] Source John McPhee, The Art of Nonfiction No. 3": Interviewed by Peter Hessler. *The Paris Review*; Spring 2010 http://www.theparisreview.org/interviews/5997/the-art-of-nonfiction-no-3-john-mcphee>.

[34] Source: Nancy Crampton, photographer, *Writers*, pp. 146-147, 220.

[35] Source: Nelson W. Aldrich, Jr., editor, *George Being George*, pp. 374-375.

[36] Source: Zia, Helen, "Review of *I Love a Broad Margin to My Life* by Maxine Hong Kingston." 27 February 2011 http://www.powells.com/review/2011_02_27.html

[37] Source: Dick King-Smith, *Chewing the Cud*, p. 41.

[38] Source: Cosmo Landesman, "In his own write: Stephen Benatar." *The Sunday Times*. 11 April 2010 http://entertainment.timesonline.co.uk/tol/arts_and_entertainment/books/article7093500.ece

[39] Source: Katherine Krohn, *Stephenie Meyer: Dreaming of* Twilight, pp. 5, 13-15, 47, 90.

[40] Source: Martha E. Rhynes, *Gwendolyn Brooks: Poet from Chicago*, pp. 50, 98.

[41] Source: Ivar Bryce, *You Only Live Once*, pp. 26-27, 101.

[42] Source: Leonard S. Marcus, compiler and editor, *The Wand in the Word: Conversations with Writers of Fantasy*, pp. 96-97.

[43] Source: Kathleen Krull, *Lives of the Writers: Comedies, Tragedies (And What the Neighbors Thought)*, pp. 45-46.

[44] Source: Joe Adamson, *Tex Avery: King of Cartoons*, pp. 123, 125-127, 182, 184.

[45] Source: Maureen Furniss, editor, *Chuck Jones Conversations*, pp. 165-166.

[46] Source: Roger Ebert, "410 East Washington Street." 21 April 2009 http://blogs.suntimes.com/ebert/2009/04/410_east_washington_street.html

[47] Source: Andrea Juno and V. Vale, publishers and editors, *Pranks! Devious Deeds and Mischievous Mirth*, pp. 103-104.

[48] Source: William J. Boerst, *Generous Anger: The Story of George Orwell*, pp. 13-14, 16, 18.

[49] Source: Catherine Reef, *Ernest Hemingway: A Writer's Life*, pp. 7-8, 12.

[50] Source: Rain Pryor, *Jokes My Father Never Taught Me: Life, Love, and Loss with Richard Pryor*, pp. 137-139, 141, 152.

[51] Source: Moe Howard, *Moe Howard and the Three Stooges*, pp. 15-18.

[52] Source: Chuck Jones, *Chuck Redux: Drawing from the Fun Side of Life*, pp. 44-46.

[53] Source: Lawrence J. Epstein, *George Burns: An American Life*, p. 71.

[54] Source: Leonard S. Marcus, compiler and editor, *Funny Business: Conversations with Writers of Comedy*, p. 79.

[55] Source: Connie Schultz, "Just for Fun, Pretend Your Next Breath Is Your Last." Creators Syndicate. 15 July 2015 http://tinyurl.com/neh95wd

[56] Source: Sam Weller, *Listen to the Echoes: The Ray Bradbury Interviews*, pp. 49-50.

[57] Source: Carl Rollyson, "More Than a Girl With a Gimmick." *Wall Street Journal*. 7 January 2011 http://online.wsj.com/article/SB10001424052748704034804576025691968347626.html?mod=WSJ_LifeStyle_LS_Book

[58] Source: Jon Scieszka, *Knucklehead: Tall Tales and Mostly True Stories About Growing Up Scieszka*, pp. 81-82, 97-98.

[59] Source: Gerald Walker, editor, *My Most Memorable Christmas*, p. 77.

[60] Source: Roy Clark, *My Life — In Spite of Myself!*, pp. 128-132.

[61] Source: Dennis R. Tuttle, *Life in the Minor Leagues*, pp. 20-27.

[62] Source: Arthur Marx, *Red Skelton*, pp. 271, 287-188.

[63] Source: V. Vale and Andrea Juno, editors. *Incredibly Strange Music, Vol. 2*, pp. 147, 149.

[64] Source: Cynthia True, *American Scream: The Bill Hicks Story*, pp. 40-41.

[65] Source: Rosanna Greenstreet, "Q&A: Hugh Dennis." *The Guardian*. 12 February 2011 <http://www.guardian.co.uk/lifeandstyle/2011/feb/12/hugh-dennis-interview>.

[66] Source: Lawrence J. Epstein, *George Burns: An American Life*, p. 62.

[67] Source: Richard Zoglin, *Comedy at the Edge: How Stand-up in the 1970s Changed America*, p. 156.

[68] Source: Don Rickles, *Rickles' Book*, p. 147.

[69] Source: Clive James, "Hollywood: A Love Story." *Atlantic*. June 2011 http://www.theatlantic.com/magazine/print/2011/06/hollywood-a-love-story/8501/

[70] Source: Gordon Irving, compiler, *The Wit of the Scots*, p. 20.

[71] Source: Anita Loos, *Kiss Hollywood Goodbye*, pp. 94-95.

[72] Source: David Frum, "Christopher Hitchens, 1949-2011." Huffington Post. 16 December 2011
http://www.huffingtonpost.ca/david-frum/christopher-hitchens-1949_b_1152895.html

[73] Source: Alison Flood, "Ruth Rendell: a life in writing." *Guardian*. 1 March 2013
http://www.guardian.co.uk/culture/2013/mar/01/ruth-rendell-life-in-writing"
http://www.guardian.co.uk/culture/2013/mar/01/ruth-rendell-life-in-writing

[74] Source: Julia Blackburn, *With Billie: A New Look at the Unforgettable Lady Day*, pp. 230-231.

[75] Source: Eric Felten, "Contract Killings on the Sets of Soaps and Sitcoms." *Wall Street Journal*. 6 May 2011

http://online.wsj.com/article/SB10001424052748703859304576305033718863452.html?mod=WSJ_ArtsEnt_LifestyleA

[76] Source: Neil Gaiman, "Popular Writers: A Stephen King interview." Neil Gaiman's Journal. 28 May 2012 http://journal.neilgaiman.com/2012/04/popular-writers-stephen-king-interview.html>. An interview with Stephen King that appeared in the UK *Sunday Times Magazine*. Source: Rebecca Stefoff, *Stephen King*, pp. 23-24, 34-35, 132-133.

[77] Source: Chris Jones, "The Honor System." *Esquire*. 17 September 2012

[78] Source: Simon Critchley, "There Is No Theory of Everything." *New York Times*. 12 September 2015
http://tinyurl.com/o9aqzl5

[79] Source: Nancy Whitelaw, *Nathaniel Hawthorne: American Storyteller*, pp. 21-23.

[80] Source: Sophia Hollander, "Breathlessly, She Swooned — and Quoted Foucault." *Wall Street Journal*. 28 June 2011 http://online.wsj.com/article/SB10001424052702304314404576412111128015484.html?mod=WSJ_LifeStyle_Lifestyle

[81] Source: Chip Heath and Dan Heath, *Made to Stick: Why Some Ideas Survive and Others Die*, pp. 75-76.

[82] Source: Chuck Jones, *Chuck Redux: Drawing from the Fun Side of Life*, pp. 149, 213-214, 227-228.

[83] Source: Mark Bauerlein, "A Solitary Thinker." *The Chronicle Review*. 15 May 2011 http://chronicle.com/article/A-Solitary-Thinker/127464/

[84] Source: Paul Provenza and Dan Dion, *¡Satiristas!: Comedians, Contrarians, Raconteurs & Vulgarians*, p. 46.

[85] Source: Joseph Harris, *Rewriting: How to Do Things with Texts*, p. 55.

[86] Source: Carl Freedman, editor, *Conversations with Isaac Asimov*, p. 143.

[87] Source: Simon Critchley, "There Is No Theory of Everything." *New York Times*. 12 September 2015
http://tinyurl.com/o9aqzl5

[88] Source: Maurice Zolotow, *No People Like Show People*, p. 281.

[89] Source: Amy Boothe Green and Howard E. Green, *Remembering Walt: Favorite Memories of Walt Disney*, pp. vii-viii. These anecdotes are from Ray Bradbury's "Foreword."

[90] Source: Gerald Nachman, *Seriously Funny*, pp. 246, 260, 263.

[91] Source: Andrew Hecht, *Hollywood Merry-Go-Round*, p. 15.

[92] Source: Juliet Rix, "Ben Okri: My family values." *The Guardian*. 26 June 2010 http://www.guardian.co.uk/lifeandstyle/2010/jun/26/ben-okri-family-values

[93] Source: Katie Couric, *The Best Advice I Ever Got: Lessons from Extraordinary Lives*, pp. 106-107.

[94] Source: Buddy Hackett, *The Truth About Golf and Other Lies*, p. 60.

[95] Source: Michael J. Rosen, editor, *Horse People: Writers and artists on the Horses They Love*, p. 66.

[96] Source: Barry Forshaw, "The real story behind *The Girl with the Dragon Tattoo*." Timesonline.co.uk. 2 May 2010 http://entertainment.timesonline.co.uk/tol/arts_and_entertainment/books/fiction/article7113874.ece

[97] Source: Nawal El Saadawi, "Egypt's radical feminist." *The Guardian*. 15 April 2010    http://www.guardian.co.uk/lifeandstyle/2010/apr/15/nawal-el-saadawi-egyptian-feminist

[98] Source: Catherine Reef, *Walt Whitman*, pp. 26, 32-33.

[99] Source: Robert E. Drennan, ed., *The Algonquin Wits*, pp. 63-64.

[100] Source: Davis Lazar, editor, *Conversations with M.F.K. Fisher*, pp. 4, 9, 19, 99-100.

[101] Source: Karen Adir, *The Great Clowns of American Television*, pp. 197, 205-206.

[102] Source: John Hind, "Interview: Benjamin Zephaniah." *The Guardian*. 18 July 2010    http://www.guardian.co.uk/lifeandstyle/2010/jul/18/benjamin-zephaniah-life-on-a-plate

[103] Source: Patti Smith, *Just Kids*, pp. 122-123.

[104] Source: Marc Dion, "I'm Casual About Mangoes Now." Creators Syndicate. 24 August 2015 http://tinyurl.com/plck4r4

[105] Source: Stephen Smith: "Quincy Jones: the day Michael Jackson's pet snake got loose in the studio." *Guardian*. 23 August 2016 <http://tinyurl.com/zj453xq>.

[106] Source: Robert E. Drennan, editor, *The Algonquin Wits*, p. 48.

[107] Source: Michael Thomas Ford, *The Little Book of Neuroses*, pp. 2-3.

[108] Source: Newspaper Guild of New York, *Heywood Broun as He Seemed to Us*, p. 13.

[109] Source: George Jessel, *Jessel, Anyone?*, pp. 107-108.

[110] Source: Jhan Robbins, *Inka Dinka Doo: The Life of Jimmy Durante*, pp. 174-175.

[111] Source: Buddy Hackett, *The Truth About Golf and Other Lies*, pp. 23, 41, 51, 67, 69.

[112] Source: Ivar Bryce, *You Only Live Once*, p. 116.

[113] Source: Jack Benny and His Daughter Joan, *Sunday Nights at Seven: The Jack Benny Story*, pp. 98-99.

[114] Source: Joseph Barbera, *My Life in 'toons: From Flatbush to Bedrock in Under a Century*, pp. 218, 250.

[115] Source: Robert E. Sherwood's "Foreword" to Nathaniel Benchley's *Robert Benchley*, p. xiv. Nathaniel Benchley, *Robert Benchley*, pp. 134-136, 141-142.

[116] Source: Catherine Reef, *Walt Whitman*, pp. 43-44, 83, 85, 124.

[117] Source: Jhan Robbins, *Inka Dinka Doo: The Life of Jimmy Durante*, pp. 18-23, 91.

[118] Source: William J. Boerst, *Generous Anger: The Story of George Orwell*, pp. 38-40, 43.

[119] Source: Darryl Littleton, *Black Comedians on Black Comedy: How African-Americans Taught Us to Laugh*, pp. 115-116, 266, 309.

[120] Source: "Angel of Mercy." *National Enquirer*. 17 December 2002 http://www.nationalenquirer.com/celebrity/angel-mercy

[121] Source: Kevin Jackson, "Lost in transformation." *Literary Review* (UK). 13 July 2013
https://literaryreview.co.uk/lost-in-transformation

[122] Source: Michael Sellers and Gary Morecambe, *Sellers on Sellers*, pp. 117-118, 123.

[123] Source: Ritch Shydner and Mark Schiff, compilers. *I Killed: True Stories of the Road from America's Top Comics*, pp. 74-76.

[124] Source: Stephen Schochet, *Hollywood Stories*, p. 182.

[125] Source: Maureen Furniss, editor, *Chuck Jones Conversations*, p. 82.

[126] Source: Alex Clark, "Caitlin Moran: 'Let's all go and be feminists in the pub.'" *Guardian*. 19 June 2011

http://www.guardian.co.uk/theobserver/2011/jun/19/caitlin-moran-feminism-interview

[127] Source: Ritch Shydner and Mark Schiff, compilers. *I Killed: True Stories of the Road from America's Top Comics*, p. 115, 131.

[128] Source: Cynthia True, *American Scream: The Bill Hicks Story*, p. 172.

[129] Source: James Montgomery Flagg, *Roses and Buckshot*, pp. 168-169.

[130] Source: Nancy Whitelaw, *Nathaniel Hawthorne: American Storyteller*, pp. 18, 99-100.

[131] Source: Dick King-Smith, *Chewing the Cud*, pp. 28, 40, 56.

[132] Source: Elizabeth Day, "Howard Jacobson: 'I write fiction. The others write crap.'" *Guardian* (UK). 8 September 2012
http://www.guardian.co.uk/theobserver/2012/sep/09/howard-jacobson-zoo-time-interview

[133] Source: Danny Thomas, *Make Room for Danny*, pp. 64-65.

[134] Source: H. Allen Smith, *How to Write Without Knowing Nothing*, p. 101.

[135] Source: Kira Cochrane, "Stephenie Meyer on *Twilight*, feminism and true love." *Guardian*. 10 March 2013
http://www.guardian.co.uk/books/2013/mar/11/stephenie-meyer-twilight-the-host

[136] Source: Larry Rohter, "Dead for a Century, Twain Says What He Meant." *New York Times*. 9 July 2010
http://www.nytimes.com/2010/07/10/books/10twain.html?pagewanted=2&ref=general&src=me

[137] Source: Herbert Block, *Herblock: A Cartoonist's Life*, pp. 33-34.

[138] Source: Sheldon Leonard, *And the Show Goes On*, pp. 82-83.

[139] Source: William J. Boerst, *Isaac Asimov: Writer of the Future*, pp. 92, 97.

[140] Source: Kinky Friedman, *'Scuse Me While I Whip This Out*, pp. 121-122.

[141] Source: Herbert Block, *Herblock: A Cartoonist's Life*, p. 172.

[142] Source: Don Knotts, *Barney Fife and Other Characters I Have Known*, p. 98.

[143] Source: Elisabeth Schwarzkopf, *On and Off the Record: A Memoir of Walter Legge*, pp. 174, 181, 186, 189-190.

[144] Source: Dick Cavett, *Talk Show: Confrontations, Pointed Commentary, and Off-Screen Secrets*, pp. 158, 196.

[145] Source: James Montgomery Flagg, *Roses and Buckshot*, pp. 64, 67-68.

[146] Source: Leo Rosten, *People I Have Loved, Known or Admired*, pp. 61, 73.

[147] Source: Roy Smiles, *Funny People: My Journey Through Comedy*, pp. 41, 58-59.

[148] Source: Paul Krugman, "Notes to Commenters." *New York Times*. 11 January 2011 <http://krugman.blogs.nytimes.com/2011/01/11/notes-to-commenters/>.

[149] Source: Jack Benny and His Daughter Joan, *Sunday Nights at Seven: The Jack Benny Story*, pp. 70-71.

[150] Source: T.F. Peterson, *Nightwork: A History of Hacks and Pranks at MIT*, p. 160.

[151] Source: Emma Brockes, "Interview with MAURICE SENDAK." *Believer Magazine*. November/December 2012
http://www.believermag.com/issues/201211/?read=interview_sendak

[152] Source: Scott Ditzler, "'Mrs. Bridge' author Evan S. Connell looks back on the writing life." McClatchy Newspapers. 28 April 2010
http://www.popmatters.com/pm/article/124729-mrs.-bridge-author-evan-s.-connell-looks-back-on-the-writing-life/

[153] Source: H.L. Mencken, "For Aspiring Editors." Letters of Note. 13 January 2012
http://www.lettersofnote.com/2012/01/for-aspiring-editors.html

[154] Source: Nelson W. Aldrich, Jr., editor, *George Being George*, pp. 127-128.

[155] Source: Wanda Rutkowska, *Famous People in Anecdotes*, p. 30.

[156] Source: Herbert Block, *Herblock: A Cartoonist's Life*, pp. 54-55.

[157] Source: Ed McMahon, *Here's Ed: Or, How to be a Second Banana*, pp. 108-109.

[158] Source: Lisa O'Kelly, "Jeff Kinney: 'I didn't think I was writing Wimpy Kid for kids' – interview." *Guardian* (UK). 10 December 2011
http://www.guardian.co.uk/books/2011/dec/11/jeff-kinney-wimpy-kid-interview

[159] Source: H. Allen Smith, *To Hell in a Handbasket*, p. 185.

[160] Source: Connie Schultz, "Another Round of Newspaper Cuts — and a Toast." Creators Syndicate. 31 July 2013
http://www.creators.com/liberal/connie-schultz/another-round-of-newspaper-cuts-and-a-toast.html

[161] Source: H. Allen Smith, *To Hell in a Handbasket*, p. 213.

[162] Source: H. Allen Smith, *To Hell in a Handbasket*, p. 213.

[163] Source: H. Allen Smith, *How to Write Without Knowing Nothing*, pp. 35-36.

[164] Source: Joseph Barbera, *My Life in 'toons: From Flatbush to Bedrock in Under a Century*, p. 174.

[165] Source: George Jessel, *Jessel, Anyone?*, pp. 15-16.

[166] Source: Gloria Klaiman, *Night and Day: The Double Lives of Artists in America*, pp. 143-144.

[167] Source: Anita Loos, *Kiss Hollywood Goodbye*, pp. 155-156, 158.

[168] Source: Ed McMahon, *Here's Ed: Or, How to be a Second Banana*, pp. 11, 337-338.

[169] Source: Richard Zoglin, *Comedy at the Edge: How Stand-up in the 1970s Changed America*, p. 31.

[170] Source: Kerrily Sapet, *Rhythm and Folklore: The Story of Zora Neale Hurston*, pp. 49, 101-102.

[171] Source: Darryl Littleton, *Black Comedians on Black Comedy: How African-Americans Taught Us to Laugh*, p. 220.

[172] Source: William J. Boerst, *Isaac Asimov: Writer of the Future*, pp. 83-84.

[173] Source: Mrs. George Jones and Tom Carter, *Nashville Wives*, pp. 139, 145-46.

[174] Source: Jamie Farr, *Just Farr Fun*, p. 312.

[175] Source: Robert Pegg, *Comical Co-Stars of Television*, pp. 214-215.

[176] Source: Maurice Zolotow, *No People Like Show People*, p. 104.

[177] Source: John O'Connell, "This much I know: Robert Harris." *The Guardian*. 11 April 2010
http://www.guardian.co.uk/lifeandstyle/2010/apr/11/robert-harris-ghost-fatherland-polanski

[178] Source: Yael Kohen, *We Killed: The Rise of Women in American Comedy*, p. 23.

[179] Source: Kathleen Krull, *Lives of the Writers: Comedies, Tragedies (And What the Neighbors Thought)*, p. 77.

[180] Source: Ed McMahon, *For Laughing Out Loud: My Life and Good Times*, p. 209.

[181] Source: Amy Boothe Green and Howard E. Green, *Remembering Walt: Favorite Memories of Walt Disney*, pp. 43, 134.

[182] Source: Mary Beard, "Do the Classics Have a Future?" *New York Review of Books*. 12 January 2012 http://www.nybooks.com/articles/archives/2012/jan/12/do-classics-have-future/?pagination=false

[183] Source: Sheldon Leonard, *And the Show Goes On*, p. 65.

[184] Source: Roger Ebert, "The Producers." 16 December 2005 http://rogerebert.suntimes.com/apps/pbcs.dll/article?AID=/20051215/REVIEWS/51213003

[185] Source: Elisabeth Schwarzkopf, *On and Off the Record: A Memoir of Walter Legge*, pp. 186, 192-196.

[186] Source: Joan Oliver Goldsmith, *How Can We Keep from Singing: Music and the Passionate Life*, pp. 128, 144.

[187] Source: Penelope Yungshans, *Prize Winners: Ten Writers for Young People*, pp. 111-112.

[188] Source: Susan Goldman Rubin, *Music was It: Young Leonard Bernstein*, pp. 32, 133.

[189] Source: Joseph Harris, *Rewriting: How to Do Things with Texts*, pp. 78-79. See "Madness Man Movie" at http://www.youtube.com/watch?v=j2w076CrRTM

[190] Source: Otto Penzler, editor, *The Lineup*, p. 38.

[191] Source: Leonard S. Marcus, compiler and editor, *Funny Business: Conversations with Writers of Comedy*, p. 5.

[192] Source: Danny Thomas, *Make Room for Danny*, p. 187.

[193] Source: Kinky Friedman, *'Scuse Me While I Whip This Out*, p. 141.

[194] Source: Susan Goldman Rubin, *Music was It: Young Leonard Bernstein*, pp. 117-118.

[195] Source: David Morgan, *Monty Python Speaks*, p. 195.

[196] Source: Penn Jillette, *God, No! Signs You May Already be an Atheist and Other Magical Tales*, pp. xv-xvi, 156-157.

[197] Source: Steve King, "Swatting Flies." *Barnes and Noble Review*. 17 September 2010
http://bnreview.barnesandnoble.com/t5/Daybook/Swatting-Flies/ba-p/3317
Also: William Golding. Nobel Lecture. 7 December 1983
https://www.nobelprize.org/prizes/literature/1983/golding/lecture/#:~:text=Then%20you%20write%20the%20same,the%20Nobel%20Prize%20

[198] Source: Donald Hall, "THANK YOU, THANK YOU." *New Yorker*. 26 October 2012
http://www.newyorker.com/online/blogs/books/2012/10/thank-you-thank-you-donald-hall-on-a-lifetime-of-poetry-readings.html#ixzz2AmTsWEv6

[199] Source: Christine M. Hill, *Gwendolyn Brooks: "Poetry is Life Distilled,"* pp. 5-8, 21-22, 29.

[200] Source: Patti Smith, *Just Kids*, pp. 137-138.

[201] Source: Nancy Crampton, photographer, *Writers*, pp. 144-145.

[202] Source: Julie Hecht, *Was This Man a Genius? Talks with Andy Kaufman*, pp. 32-35, 64, 86-87.

[203] Source: Dick Cavett, *Talk Show: Confrontations, Pointed Commentary, and Off-Screen Secrets*, pp. 115, 117.

[204] Source: Robert Ebert, "Answer Man: Absurdity at 30,000 feet."
http://rogerebert.suntimes.com/apps/pbcs.dll/section?category=ANSWERMAN. October 2, 2005.

[205] Source: Herbert Block, *Herblock: A Cartoonist's Life*, pp. 122-123.

[206] Source: Gordon Irving, compiler, *The Wit of the Scots*, p. 43.

[207] Source: Karen Adir, *The Great Clowns of American Television*, p. 161.

[208] Source: Moe Howard, *Moe Howard and the Three Stooges*, pp. 53-54.

[209] Source: Bob Bernotas, *Amiri Baraka*, pp. 41-42.

[210] Source: Martha E. Rhynes, *I, Too, Sing America: The Story of Langston Hughes*, pp. 15, 17.

[211] Source: Andrea Juno and V. Vale, publishers and editors, *Pranks! Devious Deeds and Mischievous Mirth*, p. 108.

[212] Source: Marlo Thomas, *Growing Up Laughing: My Story and the Story of Funny*, pp. 39-30.

[213] Source: Stephen Schochet, *Hollywood Stories*, p. 21.

[214] Source: Arthur Marx, *Red Skelton*, p. 15.

[215] Source: Jon Scieszka, *Knucklehead: Tall Tales and Mostly True Stories About Growing Up Scieszka*, pp. 85-87.

[216] Source: Nellie Melba, *Melodies and Memories*, pp. 229-230, 251-252.

[217] Source: Art Linkletter, *I Wish I'd Said That!*, p. 87.

[218] Source: Newspaper Guild of New York, *Heywood Broun as He Seemed to Us*, pp. 7-9, 29-30, 37.

[219] Source: Don Knotts, *Barney Fife and Other Characters I Have Known*, pp. 216-217.

[220] Source: Wanda Rutkowska, *Famous People in Anecdotes*, pp. 27-28.

[221] Source: Jim and Henny Backus, *Forgive Us Our Digressions*, pp. 156, 158-59.

[222] Source: Robert Pegg, *Comical Co-Stars of Television*, pp. 198-199. Also: "George Lindsey. Wikipedia.
https://en.wikipedia.org/wiki/George_Lindsey

[223] Source: Leonard S. Marcus, compiler and editor, *The Wand in the Word: Conversations with Writers of Fantasy*, p. 147.

[224] Source: Joe Garner, *Made You Laugh*, p. 83.

[225] Source: Betty White, *Here We Go Again*, p. 227.

[226] Source: Penn & Teller, *Penn & Teller's How to Play in Traffic*, p. 103.

[227] Source: Penelope Yungshans, *Prize Winners: Ten Writers for Young People*, p. 94.

[228] Source: Fred Allen, *Much Ado About Me*, pp. 249-253, 255-256.

[229] Source: Bob Hope, *The Road to Hollywood*, p. 22.

[230] Source: Jamie Farr, *Just Farr Fun*, pp. 82-83.

[231] Source: Gerald Walker, editor, *My Most Memorable Christmas*, pp. 74-76.

[232] Source: Joseph Epstein: "From Wit to Twit(ter)." *Commentary*. 1 January 2015
http://tinyurl.com/n8aate8

[233] Source: "Dorothy Parker, The Art of Fiction No. 13": Interviewed by Marion Capron. *The Paris Review*. 1956
http://www.theparisreview.org/interviews/4933/the-art-of-fiction-no-13-dorothy-parker

[234] Source: Leo Rosten, *People I Have Loved, Known or Admired*, p. 68.

[235] Source: Bill Crow, *Jazz Anecdotes*, p. 189.

[236] Source: Art Linkletter, *I Wish I'd Said That!*, pp. 18, 38.

[237] Source: Andrew Hecht, *Hollywood Merry-Go-Round*, p. 22.

[238] Source: "We Lived to Serve, We Served to Live: The Staff of *The Stranger* Tells Our Restaurant-Work Stories." *The Stranger* (Washington). 16 August 2011
http://www.thestranger.com/seattle/we-lived-to-serve-we-served-to-live/Content?oid=9539251

[239] Source: Katie Couric, *The Best Advice I Ever Got: Lessons from Extraordinary Lives*, pp. 11-15, 132-134.

[240] Source: Penn Jillette, *God, No! Signs You May Already be an Atheist and Other Magical Tales*, pp. 220-224.

[241] Source: Joan Oliver Goldsmith, *How Can We Keep from Singing: Music and the Passionate Life*, pp. 72-73, 84.

[242] Source: Davis Lazar, editor, *Conversations with M.F.K. Fisher*, pp. 25, 28, 55.

[243] Source: Jillian D'Onfro, "14 Quirky Things You Didn't Know About Amazon." *Business Insider*. 10 May 2014
http://tinyurl.com/lf78n7h

[244] Source: Peggy Caravantes, *Deep Woods: The Story of Robert Frost*, p. 29.

[245] Source: David Martindale, "Author Stuart Woods gives series' character the good life." McClatchy Newspapers. 21 April 2010
http://www.popmatters.com/pm/article/124346-author-stuart-woods-gives-series-character-the-good-life/

[246] Source: Jill Harness, "God Bless You, Mr. Vonnegut." Neatorama. 10 November 2012
http://www.neatorama.com/2012/11/11/God-Bless-You-Mr-Vonnegut/#more

[247] Source: Neil Gaiman and Terry Pratchett, *Good Omens: The Nice and Accurate Prophecies of Agnes Nutter, Witch*, p. 376.

[248] Source: Oliver Burkeman, "Larry David: 'I'm cranky.'" *The Guardian*. 26 June 2010
http://www.guardian.co.uk/tv-and-radio/2010/jun/26/larry-david-interview

[249] Source: Patrick Barkham, "Did you spot the hidden message?" *Guardian* (UK). 11 July 2011
http://www.guardian.co.uk/media/2011/jul/11/news-of-the-world-hidden-message

[250] Source: Yael Kohen, *We Killed: The Rise of Women in American Comedy*, p. 30.